THE BUS WE LOVED

London's Affair with the Routemaster

TRAVIS ELBOROUGH

Granta Books
London

Granta Publications, 2/3 Hanover Yard, Noel Road, London N1 8BE

First published in Great Britain by Granta Books 2005
This edition published by Granta Books 2006

A CIP catalogue record for this book
is available from the British Library.

1 3 5 7 9 10 8 6 4 2

ISBN-13: 978-1-86207-885-7
ISBN-10: 1-86207-885-8

Typeset by M Rules
Printed and bound in Great Britain
by Bookmarque Limited, Croydon, Surrey

Travis Elborough was a bookseller and is now a freelance journalist. He reviews for the *Guardian*, and has contributed to the *Sunday Times*, *Zembla* and the *Oldie*. He lives in London.

'A pocket-sized production as sleek as the vehicle it elegises' *London Review of Books*

'Heartfelt elegy to the Routemaster, as it disappears from our streets and Satan's squeezebox takes its place' *Independent on Sunday*

'His prose trots at a brisk pace. (Bite-sized chapters fit the stations of your morning commute.) *The Bus We Loved* is an attractive object, designed with the same care Douglas Scott lavished on the Routemaster' Iain Sinclair, *Guardian*

'The author adds diligent research to his obvious enthusiasm. Interviews with drivers and engineers are interspersed with a wealth of detail on the evolution of the Routemaster. This book is beautifully designed . . . You can almost smell the mustiness in the bus interior . . . Elborough is a deft writer' Bloomberg.com

'A delightful book' *Buses*

'Elborough's nostalgia for the sights and sounds that won't come again is infectious . . . You don't have to fall in love with the Routemaster quite as passionately as Elborough clearly has to feel a little more affection for than for the behemoths of bendy-buses that are pushing it aside, or to that this well-told story is one that was worth telling' *Times Literary* *ement*

gh goes further than just mourning the demise of the lovely temaster shape and its liberating hop on–hop off entryway. He lenty of feeling and personal touch into the book, but his isciplined: historical and sociological as well as anecdotal'

then a book comes along which is a complete surprise, at is. If you expect a book detailing bus fleet numbers, arage allocations then you'll be disappointed because ch more than that . . . Readable for enthusiasts, ns, tourists, anyone in fact' *Bus and Coach Magazine*

For Orla

CONTENTS

PART 2

INTRODUCTION

It's one of those modern buses where you get on at the front and give your money to the driver; much slower and harder to love than the old Routemasters with the conductor. The new ones must be cheaper to run, though, less manpower. The world looks different, more fragile, when you have in mind that everyone everywhere tries to employ as few people as possible.

Mr Phillips John Lanchester, 1998

The philosopher Ludwig Wittgenstein once asked his students to imagine a red patch. Leaving aside, for now, what inferences he intended them to draw from this thought experiment, this language game . . . imagine a red London bus. What does it look like? Is it a double decker? Does it have a rear platform you can hop on and off? Is there a conductor on board to whom you pay your fare, from whom you seek advice? Does it have cord you can pull that results in a pleasing *ding*? Could there be a half cab at the front for the driver? Do you find it hard not to reconfigure its lights, bonnet and radiator into a friendly face? Are the curves of its bodywork good enough to reach out and stroke? Could a small child, perhaps, draw a convincing representation of it? Yes? Okay, we can begin.

The Routemaster is the last of its kind. The last bus to be

built for London, by Londoners, in London. The last open-platform London bus. To many it *is* London. After 50 years, its image is famous the world over, as synonymous with the city as Big Ben, beefeaters and black cabs. (All the Bs then.)[1] It appears on picture postcards, socks, bags, tea towels, T-shirts, key rings. It's currently on the cover of three London guidebooks and the *Oxford Dictionary of London Place Names*. There are thousands of toy and model Routemasters – from the lumps of red plastic in wire bins outside the tat shops on Oxford Street to collectors' editions costing around £100 a go. A visit to the shop in London's Transport Museum in Covent Garden or to Ian Allan's outlet at Waterloo means being presented with a bewildering selection of books, videos, CDs and DVDs on the Routemaster and its various subspecies. There has been a Routemaster beer and in Blackpool there is a Routemaster Hotel run by two former London Transport bus drivers.[2] In 1999 Catherine McDermott saw fit to include the Routemaster in her Design Museum *Book of Twentieth Century Design*.[3]

---

1 I would have added Buckingham Palace but really, does anyone outside Britain have the faintest idea of what it actually looks like?

2 Disappointingly, this is an ordinary hotel full of Routemaster memorabilia rather than a guesthouse for buses.

3 An entry that must have tickled the museum's founder, Stephen Bayley. The Routemaster did not feature in his survey of industrial design *In Good Shape* (1980) and in the *Observer* in December 2001, Bayley wrote: 'it must exist somewhere, but I have yet to find an ideal bus. However, there is something clean, air-conditioned, comfortable, fast, available in a colour of your choice, intimate, economical, with lap-top power points, a personal entertainment system and that goes everywhere you want (except central Oxford and Cheltenham). Thing is, it's called a Ford Fiesta, not a Routemaster.'

Chanel, with a knowing nod to the Routemaster, launched a London Bus Red nail polish.

It is more than a bus, it was the bus we loved, probably the only public-service road vehicle any of us has ever, hand on heart, loved. It's probably the only bus many of us have ever known by its real name.

I wasn't born in London. I visited often enough but didn't settle here until I was 25. I grew up on the South Coast, a place where most people go to die. Buses, a free service for the town's elderly inhabitants, were ubiquitous but uninteresting. The town's bus depot was behind the cinema on the seafront; nearly every film I saw there, from *The Jungle Book* to *Return of the Jedi*, was accompanied by the throaty roar of diesel engines. 'Gordon's . . . *brrum, brrum* . . . alive!' The constant hiss of airbrakes can play havoc with even a child's all-too-willing capacity to suspend disbelief.

When I finally moved to the capital, I lived in Dalston and worked in a bookshop on Islington Green. I hardly ever caught the tube, rarely had to and rarely wanted to. Black cabs never featured at all. Still don't. The 38, the 19 and the 73 Routemasters shipped me – and they *did* feel like boats – back and forth from work and beyond; their routes inform my earliest impressions of the city as a resident. They defined my ambit, my city. Beck's tube map, elegant as it was, felt reductive, London as a spark plug, useful, essential, obviously; but bus maps, fascinating sprawls of vermicelli, bore more relation to the city I was encountering. London isn't, as is often pointed out, a very logical city. Piecing it together was easier above ground. My memories of some districts are intimately connected to Routemaster bus routes. When I think of being in Notting Hill, Camberwell, Bethnal Green, the numbers 7, 36 and 8 continue to spring unbidden to mind.

To me, coming from the provinces, they always seemed so sophisticated, convivial, civilized and civilizing, I guess. In a way that tube travel in London, for all that we'd like it to be, usually isn't. There was the look of them for a start. Roll-top baths in Guardsmen's red, they exuded an air of implacable, if polite, majesty. At night they glowed like lanterns; harbour lights beckoning us home. Then there were the conductors, commissionaires of the road, a reassuring presence. Like Heisenberg's uncertainty principle, their being there, watching over us all, changed everything. They were a reminder too that London was *different*. Other cities had abandoned conductors, other than for orchestras, but we were *the capital*, we were special, we deserved more. We journeyed silver service. We enjoyed the everyday human interaction that conductors provided, the familiarity of their faces, their flip remarks (the miserable sods). We enjoyed the rituals of paying the fare, the chunter of the ticket machine, the torn strips of paper that made instant bookmarks. That cord. That bell. It was school orchestra triangle *ding ding*. A comic, comforting sound.

It also seemed to me that the layout of the bus – the entrance/exit and stairs at the back, the galleys of seats – broke up the usual provincial configurations of passengers, where 'hard lads' clustered at the rear. All life was here, there and everywhere and the better for it. But it was the liberty to hop on and off, of course, that was the Routemaster's most appealing and empowering feature. Standing on the rear platform with the wind in your face, you could imagine that London really did belong to you. The open platform acknowledged the spontaneity of the city, its wealth of possibilities. (Its dangers, perhaps. But that was our choice too.) A missed bus might get stuck at the lights further on, offering another chance to hop aboard. You travelled hopefully, happily.

On 22 September 2000, Transport for London (TfL) announced that after scouring the land it had purchased an additional 24 Routemasters to supplement the London fleet. These vehicles were to be refitted with the latest, low-emission, fuel-efficient engines and refurbished 'to bring comfort levels into the 21st century'. In the mayoral elections that May, Ken Livingstone had promised, if elected, to 'start to get conductors back on buses'. Two years earlier, as the MP for Brent then seeking Labour's nomination, Livingstone had told BBC news that he thought the reintroduction of conductors was 'a priority' and that we 'should also retain the existing Routemaster fleet until a modern Routemaster can be designed'.

Four months into his term of office and Ken had 'done us proud'. The Routemasters were, it appeared, getting a fresh lease of life, and an heir. Dave Wetzel, Livingstone's bus supremo, told the *Metro* newspaper that they were a 'practical solution for central London as well as good value. We can have three refurbished and modernized Routemasters, running on the latest ultra-low sulphur diesel, for the price of one brand-new bus.' These refurbishments, the paper reported, would allow the Routemaster to be operational until 2010. Transport for London would then 'look at guaranteeing the future of open buses by developing a "child of the Routemaster".' It was pointed out that European legislation would require every London bus to be accessible to the disabled by 2017, but TfL was said to be in the 'early stages of discussions' with manufacturers about creating such a vehicle.

Five years on . . . and from where I sit typing these words I can hear a rumble – no, that's not quite right, a curious swish with an underlying bass note – of a Mercedes-Benz Citaro, a so-called 'Bendy' bus, on route 73.[4] The departure of the Routemasters from London that has been long predicted, rumoured, whispered, insinuated, planned and (in certain quarters) dreamed of is complete.

Conceived when austerity measures were in place and areas of the city wore the scars of the Luftwaffe's bombing raids, the Routemaster was originally designed by London Transport for seventeen years' service. Between 1954 and 1968, a total of 2875 were built. (The Routemaster shares its birthday with that other stylish baby boomer, the Fender Stratocaster guitar.) In 1971, London Transport confidently predicted that they'd all be off the streets by 1978. Somehow in 1981 most were still about. But by the late 1980s several hundred had done the decent thing, and shuffled, meekly, off for scrap. Others moved out of London. Sold to the newly privatized bus companies in the regions, they plied for fares in Glasgow, Dundee, Manchester, Blackpool, Southend, Carlisle and Burnley. Of the 600 or so that were left in London – in the words of Tennyson, 'Boldly they rode and well'. By 1994, the whole fleet, the majority now in private hands, had been tarted-up

---

4   And, yes, they are noisier, knocking out 92.1 decibels in comparison with the Routemasters' modest 89.6. (*Evening Standard* 30 July 2004)

and re-engined. They were good, it was said, for a further ten years.

Britannia was cool, London was swinging again. And what could be cooler and more essentially London than a Routemaster bus? They had starring roles in videos by then-fashionable bands like Blur and Pulp.[5] *Time Out* magazine put Duke Baysee, the harmonica-playing conductor of the 38 bus, at number 66 in their Top 100 Reasons to Live in the Capital (ah lists – such a millennial thing). London without Routemasters started to seem almost unthinkable once again. We'd rather have evicted the ravens from the Tower and substituted a ringtone for Big Ben. In the horror film *28 Days Later*, an overturned and abandoned Routemaster provided the most potent symbol of London's ravaging by zombies. And the year 2017 was ages away, wasn't it?

We were in denial, because we'd heard it all before. But the underlying trends, for those who bothered to follow them (and who did? – there was a second series of *Big Brother* on), were treacherous. London ordered its first £200,000 Bendys in June 2001. As *Buses* magazine observed, 'the surprise star of Coach & Bus 2001[6] was a Mercedes Benz Citaro in full London trim'.[7] 'So,' the magazine asked Peter Hendy, TfL's new Managing Director of Surface Transport, 'is the heavyweight, thoroughbred Mercedes the bus of London's future?' Hendy replied opaquely: 'The Mayor's transport strategy gives us commitment to public consultation on vehicle design. We've only just started that.' The Citaro was, he said, 'an example of a reasonably well-developed

---

5   In two promos by Blur, in fact, *For Tomorrow* and *Parklife. Disco 2000* for Pulp.
6   An annual trade show.
7   *Buses* No. 564, March 2002.

vehicle design'. Before joining TfL in 2001, Hendy had been a
deputy director of First Group, the company which had introduced the Citaro to Manchester. We should have seen the signs.

In May 2002, Dick Halle, the strategy director for London,
advised the trade journal *Transit* that 'the Routemaster will be
phased out beyond 2004 . . . Bus services are expanding so fast
that there won't be enough of the old vehicles for the existing
Routemaster routes anyway.' And Ken's conductors? The case for
their widespread return, TfL felt after trials, was 'not proved . . .
any small gains in journey speed are insufficient to justify the
additional costs involved, and security improvements are being
made to London buses through other schemes such as closed-
circuit television.'

Nine months later, and buy-before-you-board Bendys were
sharing a corridor through the city – route 36, from Paddington
to New Cross – with Routemasters. In a survey undertaken by the
market research firm Outlook for TfL, 'the new articulated buses
achieved higher ratings on all key performance criteria compared
with Routemaster or double-deck buses.' (But who were these
people who rated 'the number of seats' on a 49-seater Bendy at
8.5 and in a 72-seater Routemaster at 7.4?) In April 2003, TfL
revealed that it would be withdrawing Routemasters from three
of the remaining 20 routes by the end of that year.

Covering the story, *Buses* magazine reported that: 'The word
on the grapevine is that some senior London bus company managers are complaining that their RMLs[8] are increasingly expensive

---

8 The longer 72-seater Routemasters.

to maintain and that they are attracting a disproportionate number of claims from passengers involved in platform accidents.' The *Guardian* on 26 September 2004 noted that an American lawyer had sought compensation of more than £3 million after falling off a Routemaster in Putney High Street and suffering brain damage. David Brown, the chief executive of the bus operator Go-Ahead, was quoted as saying: 'Thirty years ago when a passenger fell off the back it wouldn't have crossed their minds to seek litigation. Now it is the second thing they do after receiving treatment.'

On 29 April 2004, by which time six Routemaster routes had already been quietly (sneakily?) spirited away, TfL confirmed in an article in *Metro* that any buses that were 'inaccessible' to 'wheelchair users and parents with buggies' would be 'replaced before the end of 2005'. And that, as they say, was that. No further arguments would be brooked. The Routemaster was abruptly to disappear.

This book is an attempt to tell its story; more hagiography than history perhaps, a fond farewell to a soon-to-be-absent friend from a grateful passenger. My debt to the many books already published on the Routemaster is enormous. But my interests are cultural rather than technical. A bus is nothing without people, after all. Purists will have to forgive a rather *laissez-faire* attitude to the numerous bus types and a general absence of fleet numbers, codes and the like.

I wanted to see how this bus fitted into London's own story, how events in the city shaped its destiny, what its passing might mean. Why was it the last *real* London bus? What were its origins? Who could design and build a bus that could last half a century? A bus that is admired in distant parts of the world. A bus we loved. A bus, the like of which we'll probably never see again.

PART I

BIRTHPLACE

It's difficult to avoid the colour yellow at Chiswick Park: yellow panels with maps and information on them, wardens in yellow shirts and jackets, yellow rubbish bins that demand, 'Please feed me'. What kind of yellow? A perky kind: the yellow of sou'westers, rubber ducks, toy hammers, *Tour de France* winner jerseys and the dust jackets of Victor Gollancz novels. The colour suits the idea of this place, 556 Chiswick High Road, as a 'business park' or 'complex'.

An ornamental lake runs through the middle of the site. Piles of pinky-white stones and trees and clumps of rushes line its banks. A scrawny metal and concrete bridge connects the opposing sides about three-quarters of the way along, before the main lake peters out into a rockery. Beyond, a further expanse of water contains Koi carp. The ambience is self-consciously oriental, very

Zen, but the greens, russets and browns of the vegetation bring to
mind the Thames at Strand on the Green half a mile away. Turner
at Brentford.

Designed by the Richard Rogers Partnership, Chiswick Park
bills itself as 'a revolutionary place to work'. It does not, or so its
website insists, have 'tenants', it has 'guests'. The website's home-
page springs into action with a quote from Douglas Adams: 'I love
deadlines. I like the whooshing sound they make as they fly by.'
And here indeed, are all the estate agents, marketing consultants
and telephone engineers – Foxtons, TeleText, One.Tel, Empower
Interactive – that Adams had the rulers of the planet Golga-
frincham blast into the darkest recesses of outer space.

Chiswick Park, as the commercial letting bumf I'd taken with
me proclaimed, 'benefits from excellent transport links'.
Heathrow was 15–30 minutes away, the M4 was 'on the
doorstep', one tube station lay opposite the gates, another two
tube stations were 'a short walk away'. Buses? It seemed that
nobody here needed to know anything about them, either as a
current means of transport or as the history of this part of
Chiswick. There was nothing – no discreetly placed plaque or
heritage sign, not even the usual quasi-ironic bar or café name –
to indicate that for more than 60 years Chiswick Park was home
to Chiswick bus works. Forget the yellow; the big colour in these
parts used to be red.

When the works opened in 1922, the London General Omnibus
Company could boast that it was 'an unmistakable landmark'. It
extended over 31 acres; the main building occupied 300,000
square feet. 'There is no motor repair shop in the world that can

The entrance to Chiswick works in 1954.

justly be compared with this enterprise,' the General maintained.
'When in full swing, the works give employment to something
like 2000 people, the men being almost equally divided between
the engineering and the coach-building sections.' Three thousand
motor buses that carried 'Londoners . . . to almost every important market town or village within a 30-mile radius of central
London' were serviced here in the 1920s, and there was an
experimental engineering shop that developed bespoke vehicles
for the company. In 1925, the Chiswick Training School was
established to tutor drivers and conductors joining the General,
and to retrain existing staff whenever its engineers introduced
new models.

With the creation of the London Transport Passenger Board in 1933, London General was subsumed by London Transport, and Chiswick Works became the hub of the largest bus undertaking in the entire world. London Transport's catchment stretched out, with Greenline and Country bus services, into a 2000-square-mile area that encompassed swathes of Hertfordshire, Buckinghamshire, Essex, Surrey and Kent. Each day its buses carried 9½ million passengers. For the next 20 years, the majority of London's buses were designed, repaired and maintained here and London bus drivers continued to be tested on Chiswick's infamous 'skidpan' until well into the 1980s.

It was at Chiswick that the Routemaster bus was born.

The works closed in 1990, just as plans to privatize London Transport were published and the capital's routes primed for tender. All of its buildings were eventually demolished. There really is nothing to see here. *Nada*. Amid all the yellow, I found it utterly impossible to conjure up an image of rows of smart blood-red buses filing out to their garages. For want of anything better to do and because it seemed appropriate, I boarded a number 440 bus heading for Stonebridge Park. As I ambled on, a woman in front of me was berating the driver. 'Why they take so long? I've been waiting over an hour for this bus. I wait and wait,' she shouted at a Perspex window from which apologetic noises emanated. I heard 'road works' and 'diversions' mentioned. 'Not good enough,' the woman said, as she scurried inside and grabbed a seat, huffing and puffing for effect, as she went.

The bus was a dull, if nippy, single decker. I'd noticed that it bore logos for 'London United' and 'TransDev Group' on its front, a pseudo regal crown for United and for TransDev, a weird, ECG screen blip of green and blue. Later, when I returned home, I had a quick google and found that they were 'an international transport group' based in Paris with experience of 'managing and developing transport networks' in 'Strasbourg, Nantes and Grenoble'. With London buses, France is always a good place to start.

2

OMNES OMNIBUS

The Omnibus was tried in about 1800, with four horses and six
wheels; but we refused to accept it in any shape till we imported
the fashion from Paris in 1830.

Volume of Varieties C Knight, 1850

Near to Biba in Kensington, Lee Bender's Bus Stop was one of
London's hippest boutiques in the early 1970s – a scarlet temple
to man-made fibres and op-art prints. Quizzed on the name,
Bender once claimed, 'We chose the name "Bus Stop" because it
was so identifiably British.' And yet the bus is a quintessentially
French invention.[9] The mathematician Blaise Pascal drew up in

9 As incidentally, is the Hackney cab; derived from the French *haquenée* (an
   ambling nag rather than the London borough), it was pioneered by Captain

the 1650s what is believed to be Paris's earliest public carriaging scheme – shortly after Pascal was nearly dashed off a bridge at Neuilly in a coaching accident. In March 1662 it was put into practice. Specially designed 8-seater vehicles started to carry across the city members of the aristocracy and bourgeoisie, the only classes permitted by law to ride in them (soldiers, servants and artisans were excluded). But the rich quickly grew tired of the novelty, the carriages ceased to ply, and the idea seems to have lain dormant for 150 years until it was revived in Nantes in western France.

In or about 1826, one Stanislas Baudry, a former medical student and retired French army officer, opened what he hoped would be a lucrative steam bathing venture beside his flour mill at Richebourg on the city's edge. (The mill generated the vapours for the baths.) Business proved slack. To encourage custom he offered a coaching service to take would-be bathers who had been put off by the distance from the centre of Nantes; he could hardly move the mill, after all. His coaches (*Les Voitures des Bains de Richebourg*) soon attracted passengers who had no intention of bathing but found them a cheap and convenient means to traverse the city. Baudry had accidentally found a new career.

He gave up the baths (the mill's fate is not recorded), acquired two 16-seater coaches and obtained permission from the municipality to operate a public transport business. By chance, or so

---

Baily or Bailey, an old sea dog who'd served under Sir Walter Raleigh. Possibly the same Captain Bailey who, after quarrelling with Raleigh over the spoils from a captured French vessel on the great mariner's last, fateful voyage to America in 1617, turned back for Plymouth in a huff.

the story goes, Baudry's carriages terminated near a milliner's run by a Monsieur Omnes whose shop sign featured a Latin pun on his surname – *Omnes omnibus*, All for everyone. Whether Baudry adopted it as a slogan encapsulating the inclusivity of his new enterprise, or whether it was a contraction of 'at the sign Omnibus', the word started to be applied to the coaches themselves. Within two years, Baudry was running omnibuses in Bordeaux and had formed the *Entreprise Générale des Omnibus* in Paris, creating a network of routes serving the French capital. His success, however, provoked fierce competition in the city. Driven to the edge of bankruptcy by rival Parisian operators, he committed suicide in 1830. Not by throwing himself under a bus. He chose to dive into the Seine.

George Shillibeer was the man who brought Baudry's ideas across the Channel. Perhaps if he had stayed in Paris for a little longer he might have gained a hint of Baudry's difficulties. As it was, he witnessed only the boom and was destined to repeat many of the Frenchman's mistakes. Having retired from the Royal Navy and, if some of the gamer accounts of his life are to be believed, after a spell as a brandy smuggler, Shillibeer learnt coachbuilding in London. In 1825, at the age of 28, he went to Paris and established a coach business there, possibly producing some vehicles for *Messagerie Générale de France, Lafitte & Caillard*, the dominant stagecoaching company in northern France. When the first omnibus companies began operating in the city, Shillibeer gained a commission to fashion a longer-bodied coach suitable for their needs. It dawned on him that the same type of coach and service could work equally well in London. He sold the French concern and, in partnership with a John Cavell, set up a livery stable and coachworks in premises on Bury Street, Bloomsbury.

There was, however, one not insignificant hurdle to running omnibuses in London: Hackney coachmen possessed a complete monopoly in the busy central districts. Congestion was a fear – even then – and stagecoaches, including those journeying short distances across the city, could pick up or set down passengers only at designated points, usually inns, within the hundred or so inner parishes. Shillibeer's omnibus 'on the Parisian mode' wasn't technically a stagecoach but it looked unlikely to escape the ruling. Drawn by three bay horses harnessed abreast and commodious enough to take 18 passengers inside, it was an eye-catching, wide, boxy structure with a flat roof, windows on three sides and a door and ladder at the rear. The chances of it heading into what De Quincey called 'the Great Mediterranean of Oxford Street' unnoticed were slim, and it was probably too wide for some of the City's narrow thoroughfares. Rather than squabble with the authorities, Shillibeer plumped for a route from Paddington to the Bank, which was then the northern edge of London, which he felt would attract enough trade from the new breed of affluent suburban dwellers for a viable service.

Industrialization, which had unpicked the traditional relationships between work and home, was gradually making travel a daily feature of urban life. Mimicking the country estates of aristocrats, wealthier merchants, who could afford to maintain a horse and carriage, increasingly chose to live in the suburbs. Their habits were copied by the nascent middle classes, the traders and clerks. The New Road (now the Marylebone, Euston, Pentonville

and City Roads) was London's first bypass. An initiative put
through Parliament by the Duke of Grafton – despite objections
from the Duke of Bedford in Bloomsbury – it was primarily
intended to steer cattle bound for Smithfield away from the
centre. Begun in 1757 and completed in the following year, it suc-
cessfully linked the previously isolated villages of Paddington and
Islington. (The Grand Junction Canal would not reach
Paddington until 1801, and the railway not until 1838.) For a
while the road endured as a kind of perimeter fence, a *here be
yokels* boundary line between the burgeoning town and the country. However, the construction of Pentonville (the Gallic 'ville' a
gauchely *nouveau* touch) in the 1770s and Somers Town some
years later brought the town north and, as suburban develop-
ments continued to extend, the road closer into town. Already
patronized by short-stage stagecoaches, the New Road had, from
Shillibeer's point of view, the distinct advantage of passing outside the cabmen's fiefdom.

Despite objections from local residents, Shillibeer's omnibus –
the word painted prominently down its side – embarked on its
maiden voyage from outside the Yorkshire Stingo public house in
Paddington on 4 July 1829. At the helm as driver and conductor,
resplendently dressed in uniforms, were the sons of two naval
officers. (Presumably, old chums of Shillibeer.) The fare for the
full journey to Bank was 1s 6d for passengers sitting inside (periodicals provided gratis) and 1s for those who sat on top. Unlike
with the short-stage coaches there was no advance booking; passengers could just turn up, pay and go, and the omnibus ran at
advertised times, every 2–3 hours.

They were a hit and competitors were not slow off the mark.

Shillibeer's omnibus 'on the Parisian mode'.

By 1831, 57 omnibuses were running on the Paddington to Bank route, and passengers could now catch a ride every 2–3 minutes. The following year, the Hackney cabmen's monopoly on central London ended when the Stage Coach Act abolished stopping restrictions on coaches. From St Alban's Place on the Paddington side of Edgware Road, Shillibeer launched his assault on the town with a new service along Oxford Street to the City. Soon however, as with Baudry in Paris, Shillibeer found it increasingly difficult to keep pace with the competition. Even though the more established operators had already banded together, forming a voluntary association to keep pirates at bay and regulate the trade, a certain dog-eat-dog atmosphere flourished.[10] New

10   One less successful entrant to the ring was a steam-powered coach introduced

operators, using lighter and faster vehicles, merciless in their pursuit of custom, were gradually edging Shillibeer off the road. The era of a conductor as a nautical popinjay was over, now 'cads' who could 'chuck an old gen'lm'n into the buss, shut him in, and rattle off, afore he knows where it's a-going to', as Dickens observed in *Sketches by Boz*, roamed the highways.

In 1834, evidently tiring of the fight, he left the New Road business to an associate, William Morton, and devoted his energies to a fresh scheme; an omnibus service from Greenwich to the West End. His choice of route, on this occasion, couldn't have been worse. The first bricks for a viaduct to carry London's first railway, the London and Greenwich, were being laid. The line from London Bridge to Deptford was completed in 1836, and reached Greenwich two years later. As if to further underline the arrival of the steam age, the route was also served by a steamboat on the Thames. It all proved too much for Shillibeer, who went bankrupt trying to compete and spent a period in a debtor's gaol. He surfaced to patent, to little interest, a combined hearse and carriage in 1841, and ran an undertaking business near Bunhill Fields offering 'Catholic fittings from Paris'.

A photograph of him taken late in life captures a portly gent with mutton chop whiskers, the remaining hanks of hair at each side of his head greased forward into two giant Byronic swoops like a bat's wings. He doesn't look particularly happy but then

---

to the New Road in the summer of 1833 by Walter Hancock and The London and Paddington Steam Carriage Co. The public were never entirely convinced of its safety – they feared, with some grounds, that the boiler might explode – and the vehicle made its last journey three years later.

who does in Victorian photographs? It wasn't really the aesthetic
or the point. These things cost money and few had the patience
or the teeth for smiling. (Think of Oscar Wilde. That enigmatic
tight-lipped, Mona Lisa grin, hiding teeth blackened by mercury
treatments for syphilis.) 'Disgruntled' is a word that tends to crop
up in summaries of Shillibeer's latter years – and who could
blame him if he was. And yet he supported good causes: one of
his final acts was to ensure 50 acres of Hainault Forest, near to his
home in Chigwell, were preserved for a public recreation ground.

When he died in 1866, aged 69, most of London's major rail
stations were complete, the opening stage of the Metropolitan,
the world's first underground railway, was in business, and, the
spiffingly named American eccentric George Francis Train had
laid an experimental tram rail in the city. The London omnibus,
Shillibeer's own legacy, was now an institution, albeit one that
he'd failed to profit from.[11] He might, perhaps, have expected his
name to live on after his death. As Hoover is with vacuum
cleaner, 'Shillibeer' did for a while become virtually synonymous
with 'omnibus' and looked highly likely to supplant it. Alas, it was
not to be. Although in November 1862, a London journal called
Leisure Hours did maintain that in New York 'Shillibeer' remained
the preferred term, there is little evidence to support this claim.
'Omnibus' appears pretty frequently Stateside from the 1830s
onwards. Washington Irving, a New Yorker, used it in reference to
Britain's Reform Bill in 1831. In London, Shillibeer's name is

11   Shillibeer did, nonetheless, live long enough to see many of his former adver-
     saries gobbled up by a French invader, the *Compagnie Générale des Omnibus
     de Londres* (see page 17). Which must, surely, have come as some consolation.

preserved by a pub in Islington and a stubby dead end off the Marylebone Road close to where his omnibus enterprise began.

One August day in 2004, I had a look at this little street, Shillibeer Place W1, and encountered there a group of teenage boys, all baseball caps, sloppy tracksuit pants and broken centres of gravity, and a familiar, pungent aroma. Lounging about on the pavement next to a row of new flat conversions, ersatz Neo-Georgian ('where the contemporary meets the classical' read the estate agent's board), the boys were taking advantage of the alley's seclusion to indulge in a smoke. It seemed apt, in a way. 'Getting on the bus' was a euphemism Dom, an old hippie friend of mine, Hawkwind's *Quark, Strangeness and Charm* invariably cued up on his stereo, employed for getting stoned. A native of Sutton Coldfield, he pronounced bus 'buzz', loading the word with narcotic significance. One of the boys, I realized, was in the process of skinning up. Sitting on the tarmac, Rizla papers laid out on his knees, he was constructing a fresh joint with all the care and love of an Airfix modeller at work on the undercarriage of a Sopwith Camel. We exchanged glances. I tried to give a nod, and then shuffled off in the direction of Paddington station, pausing, to their evident amusement, to photograph the street sign as I left.

The London omnibus boom continued unabated in the 1840s ('Omnibus Nuisance' became a familiar newspaper phrase throughout the decade) but finally reached its peak in 1851 with the Great Exhibition. The Exhibition attracted more than six million visitors – the population of England and Wales was then just shy of 18 million. Such an influx of visitors to Hyde Park led to a further expansion of omnibus services, and to take more

passengers per bus proprietors took to bolting wooden benches, 'knife-boards' as the wags at *Punch* christened them, to the roofs of their vehicles. And so the top deck was born.

Across the Channel meanwhile, omnibus services in Paris had merged into a single, highly profitable organization, the *Compagnie Générale des Omnibus* – a state-sanctioned private monopoly. Leopard Foucaud, Parisian businessman, and Joseph Orsi, a French *émigré* with a keen, touching-on-the-vampiric interest in the London bus scene, were convinced that the same idea would work in London. They began approaching London operators with the aim of creating a public company. The idea of a unified bus service for London was given further impetus by the establishment in 1855 of the Metropolitan Board of Works – a forerunner of the London County Council – and the first city-wide authority. In the same year, Foucaud, Orsi and their English partners formed the *Compagnie Générale des Omnibus de Londres* and began accumulating a commanding share of the capital's business by buying out several individual bus proprietors, together with their vehicles and horses. Six hundred buses were acquired in this way in the first year of operation.

Trading under the anglicized London General Omnibus Company, the company had a London office at 454 West Strand, but its headquarters remained in Paris at 14 rue Vivienne. While *The Times* looked favourably on this Anglo-French venture, assuring its readers that fares would be cheaper in the long run, opposition was fierce and a campaign aimed at 'keeping the

Frenchies out' widely endorsed. Such anti-French sentiment finally persuaded the company to 'naturalize' itself in 1858 and to reregister permanently in the English name.

Having inherited a rag-tag of vehicles and staff, the company embarked on a series of initiatives which markedly improved London's bus services. It held a competition for an ideal bus in 1856, awarding £100 to a Hammersmith coachbuilder called R F Miller. By 1858, three-quarters of its fleet consisted of new or improved vehicles. It introduced a sixpenny 'correspondence' ticket, enabling passengers to transfer from one line of buses to another without extra charge, though they failed to catch on and were withdrawn after a couple of years. To eradicate badly behaved conductors, it recruited soldiers returning from the Crimean war. 'By the introduction of what is military,' said *Punch*, 'we shall have at last attained to what is civil.' Its efforts were applauded by *All the Year Round*, the periodical founded by Dickens. 'I am bound to say that in many respects the omnibuses and their men are greatly improved during my experience . . . by the salutary rule of the London General Omnibus Company . . . the omnibus servants, the coachmen and conductors, from insolent blackguards have become, for the most part, civil and intelligent men, while the whole "service" – horses, harness, food etc – has been placed on a greatly improved footing.'

Foucaud had always nursed grand ambitions for the *Générale*. At its inception he drafted plans to coordinate all public road and steamboat travel in the capital – including the tramways, when built. He didn't live to see it, and such a scheme for centralization would not come to pass until the formation of London Transport in the 1930s, but his dreams took one step closer to being fulfilled

in 1908 when the company gained a near monopoly of bus services in London. For the remainder of the 19th century the
General worked fairly harmoniously with other operators, such as
the Peckham-based Thomas Tilling, even adopting a roll-ticketing
system invented by the rival London Road Car Company.

What transformed the London bus landscape, however, were
the electric trams – and the motorbus.

Like that of the motor car, the motorbus's development had been
hopelessly stifled by the Road Locomotive Act, which restricted
all mechanically propelled vehicles to a speed of two miles an
hour in towns and, lest any pedestrians be harmed, required a
man with a red flag to walk in front of the vehicles at all times.
The Act was repealed in 1896. From 1897 to the end of 1904 the
Metropolitan Police issued 80 motorbus licences, though at the
beginning of 1905 there were still only 20 motorbuses working in
London compared to 1400 horse buses. By the end of that year,
however, about 230 motorbuses were in operation.[12] At the fore-
front of this change were Thomas Tilling and the London Motor
Omnibus Company Ltd. Trading as Vanguard, and originally
based in a John Nash building near Regent's Park that had once
housed a Booth's gin distillery, it forged ahead with petrol buses,
improving the standards of vehicles by setting up a main overhaul
works on Black Horse Lane in Walthamstow.[13]

---

12 In 1907, a leading chemist publicly stated that he believed that motorbus
    fumes by killing off flies and insects were making London a healthier place.
13 The Vanguard also has the dubious distinction of being involved in Britain's
    first major motorbus accident. A Vanguard bus on a trip to Brighton crashed
    on Handcross Hill in Sussex killing 10 people in 1906.

The Routemaster's story effectively begins with what happened next. In July 1908, the General took over both Vanguard and the London Road Car Company, and later, in 1911, the Great Eastern of London. Now the dominant force in London and having assumed Vanguard's technical expertise, the General was in a position to fashion its own buses rather than purchase them from manufacturers. A new subsidiary, Associated Equipment Company, based in Vanguard's Walthamstow works, was formed. With the General's chief engineer Frank Searle in charge, the company would develop buses tailor-made for London and build chassis for other operators. The first fruits of this arrangement, the X-type, a 34-seat double decker, appeared on 12 August 1909. It was followed a year later by an improved model, the B-type, which became the world's first mass production bus. Cro-Magnon man to the Routemaster's *Homo sapiens*, if you will. ('B is the useful ubiquitous Bus, a good way to travel for you and for us', as a General advertisement put it.)

Like many of the early motorbuses, the B-type still looked as though someone had rustled the horse from the front end. There was no windscreen; it had solid tyres, an open staircase and its top-deck passengers – and the driver – travelled *al fresco*. (The General supplied its drivers with caps and jackets for the first time this year, which at least did something to mitigate the cold and the wet.) But with a 30-horse-power engine and 3-speed gears, the 34-seater B-type was a big step forward. More than 1000 were in service by 1911. The last General horse bus – the route from London Bridge to Moorgate – ran on the 25 October that year.

In 1912, after several months of negotiations, the Underground Electric Railways under the exemplary leadership of Albert Stanley (subsequently ennobled to Baron Ashfield of Southwell in 1920) assumed ultimate control of London General. Ashfield, born plain Albert Knattriess in Derby in 1874, had emigrated to Detroit with his parents as a child. (Pater Knattriess, in keeping with generations of migrants to America, had grown bored with having the spelling and pronunciation of the family name mangled and changed it to Stanley in 1897.) After taking a job with the Detroit Street Railway as a teenager, Stanley progressed through the company to become its general superintendent. In 1903 he joined New Jersey Tramways. He was poached for the Underground at the suggestion of the company's American shareholders in 1907 and made managing director in 1910.

Stanley's first action as MD was to amalgamate the three separate tube lines – the Hampstead, Piccadilly and Bakerloo – into a single concern. He then sought to buy up its competitors and by 1913 the Underground Group – known as 'the Combine' – possessed the lion's share of London's bus services, a slither of the tram network and, with the exception of the Metropolitan and the Waterloo and City Line, the complete Underground system.

This wide-ranging portfolio enabled the group to coordinate its efforts in the capital; the General's buses began calling at suburban and central Underground stations, enhancing journeys into and around central London for commuters. By the start of the First World War, the company had extended its reach into the outer suburbs, running services into Middlesex, Surrey, Essex and Berkshire. More than 2000 General B-types were in circulation –

1300 of them soon to be sent to France to work as troop carriers on the Western Front.[14]

Although many B-types returned unscathed when the hostilities ended, the General was left with a war-weary and depleted fleet. In 1919, the company started to modernize its stock of vehicles, bringing in a new bus it had devised with AEC. The K-type marked another ladder rung in London bus design. Instead of placing the driver directly behind the engine, on the K-type they were positioned beside it – a style that persisted into the Routemaster era. Putting the driver and engine side by side at the front allowed the General to increase the capacity of its buses – the K could carry 46 passengers and, following on quickly behind the K, a larger S-type bus could seat 54.

The K and the S were open toppers; the Metropolitan Police nervous that covered top decks would cause crashes. The Met relented in 1925, and the General responded by fixing rooftops to its latest NS double deckers. This 'all weather' NS class also boasted dropped body frames, which lowered their centres of gravity, bringing their rear platforms nearly level with the pavement. Londoners, for the first time, could hop on and off the back with ease.

*

14   On 15 February 1920, B43, 'Old Bill of the Menin Road', and 40 'veteran' driv-
      ers were presented to King George V in the quadrangle of Buckingham Palace.
      The King, as he shook hands with the men and inspected the vehicle, was over-
      heard telling one of his palace staff that while he had been inside a tramcar this
      was his first time aboard an omnibus. Reporting on the ceremony for the
      Evening News, the suspense writer and occultist Arthur Machen wondered if,
      in recognition of its service to the nation, B43 shouldn't be 'honourably sta-
      tioned, in the manner of [Nelson's] *Victory*, a noble monument to all omnibus
      men, as the *Victory* is the glory of the sea'.

The Roaring Twenties were a trying period for the General. Its pre-eminence was suddenly challenged by an explosion of free-booting pirate bus operators in London. The trend had been fired off by a trio of London cabbies, led by Mr A G Partridge, who had discovered a legal loophole. Partridge realized that as long as the vehicle and the routes it adhered to were approved by the Metropolitan Police, there was no specific limit on the number of routes a firm could operate. A company with only a single bus could therefore pitch up on different routes at different times of the day, cherry picking customers when trade was busiest. Partridge and his partners sold their cabs, purchased a Leyland bus and began smuggling their 'Chocolate Express' (it was painted brown) on to the General's turf. This enterprising scam was quickly copied and by the mid-1920s, there were estimated to be over 200 pirate buses in London – one trading, fleetingly, as the London Genial Omnibus Co.

The pirates' cause was championed by the leftist *Daily Herald* newspaper, which rallied behind the underdogs against what they characterized as a bullyboy Combine,[15] and by the right-wing *Daily Telegraph*, which believed that 'room for all' competition would lead to better services and reduced fares. Fares did drop for a time and passengers in the central area weren't short of buses. But the situation on the streets was frequently chaotic. Rival companies sabotaged each other's vehicles and racing buses alarmed their passengers.

Stanley, now Baron Ashfield, had long defended the Combine's position, branding competition 'a dangerous weapon'. The General,

15   The General could be ruthless. The Chocolate Express was hounded by the

it was stated, would have no option but to cut its loss-making services if the independents persisted in skimming the cream. The trade journal *Modern Transport* came down on the General's side, arguing that 'there must be no risk of a sparsity of services on the rim and a glut at the hub' and advocating a single transport undertaking for London. Ashfield had himself called for 'a responsible judicial authority' to prevent London falling victim to unbridled competition.

The excesses of bus brigandry were quelled by the passing of the London Traffic Act, which came into force in 1925. Under this legislation, the Ministry of Transport was empowered to designate the maximum number of buses in certain restricted areas. Schedules and routes had to be lodged with the police and new operators were effectively barred from joining the fray. Shorn of its freedom, independent operation became less viable, and the General and its associates soon snaffled up the smallest independent operators – most were gone by late 1920s.

'Competition,' Ashfield had also maintained, 'ends in obsolete vehicles being retained in service when they should have reached the scrap heap.' Having now seen off (or bought out) the pirates, the General funnelled its resources into a trinity of new AEC chassied buses: a single-decker T-bus for its suburban 'Country' routes, a 6-wheeled LT double decker (nicknamed 'Bluebirds' because of their blue moquette seat covers), and a 4-wheeled ST double decker with an enclosed staircase.

General's buses everywhere it went to begin with. When this failed to deter Partridge and the other pirates, the company marshalled 1000 extra buses on to the streets in an attempt to drive them out of business.

The company, along with AEC, had also started to trial diesel engines, and these experiments eventually evolved into the first mass-produced diesel bus – a 4-wheeled double decker called the STL. A sort of bastard child of the ST and the LT, it was a jumble of both buses even down to its three-letter name. Although it lacked finesse to begin with (the design was smartened up through the 1930s), it was relatively modern in appearance. That's 'modern' in the sense that you could see it enjoying tea and cucumber sandwiches, a sherry later in the day in an engine shed with the Reverend Awdry's Edward, Gordon and Henry. It had a large, sit-up-and-beg front radiator, an enclosed staircase, a rear platform with a pole, and an upper deck that extended over the top of the driver's cab, allowing more seats upstairs. In the genealogy of London buses, you'd probably finger it as the Routemaster's great uncle, the suave elderly bachelor with the fondness for vintage wines and a cheroot perennially on the go. (In profile, some of the later STL models look remarkably Routemaster-esque.) The STL became a London standard and tarried in the capital for the next two decades.

The pirate debacle had only sharpened the clamour, among interested parties at least, for transport to be integrated in London. Ashfield, on behalf of the Underground Group, lobbied for a legislated private monopoly. However in May 1929, Ramsay MacDonald formed the second Labour government and appointed the charismatic and egotistical Herbert Morrison as Minister for Transport. Morrison, the Lambeth-born son of a policeman, was opposed to the idea of a private body and proposed instead a government-appointed public board to manage London's bus, tram and Underground services.

Morrison would be swept from office with the fall of the Labour administration in 1931, but his London Passenger Bill, thrashed out with Ashfield earlier that year, survived and in modified form received Royal assent two years later.

The London Passenger Transport Act was passed in March 1933. The act created the London Passenger Transport Board, the largest transport organization in the world. Rather than a private monopoly or a government-appointed body, the board was to be an independent public corporation with trustees on the lines of the BBC. This guaranteed a level of independence from government meddling while, thanks to a government works programme, assuring vital investment from the Treasury – a winning combination that would lead to a golden age in London's transport history and resulted in an integrated network that was, for a time, without equal in the world.

Ashfield, it was unanimously agreed, would chair this new board, with Frank Pick, the formidable managing director of the Underground Group, as vice-chairman and chief executive. On 1 July 1933, the London Passenger Transport Board officially came into being and the London General Omnibus Company, after 77 years, ceased to exist.

3

THE BLESSED PICK

London owes Frank Pick a great deal. The red, white and blue roundel of the Underground's logo; the clear and distinct Johnson typeface of its signage; Harry Beck's diagrammatic tube map; the architecture of Charles Holden's incomparable Piccadilly Line stations: all of them were instigated by Frank Pick. He bequeathed to London an entire civic identity that it could be proud of. (Who can honestly say, as they ride up the escalator into Holden's grand, circular concourse at Piccadilly Circus, that they have not at one point in their lives felt underdressed for the absence of a rakish hat and underprovisioned for the lack of a large dry martini in one hand as they strode toward the ticket barriers?[16] You can still see that when

---

16   Perhaps not the effect that Holden and Pick, both teetotallers were after, but I'm sure they'd approve of the sentiment.

it opened in 1928 its elegance and modest splendour would have been the equal of anything above ground.) There are few cities in the world whose sense of self is so intricately bound up with the iconography of its public transport utility – possibly because it is (or was) such a beacon of order in a disorderly and haphazard metropolis.

As the Underground Group's publicity and traffic development manager, and then as its managing director, Pick brought coherence, crisp modernity and uncompromising standards to every aspect of the service – championing modern art in platform posters[17] and remodelling ticket halls and building stations in strikingly contemporary and continental styles. In 1942 the architectural historian Nikolaus Pevsner called Pick 'the Lorenzo the Magnificent of our age' and pronounced him 'the greatest patron of the arts whom this century has so far produced in England'.

One of his boldest architectural commissions was for the company's headquarters at 55 Broadway. Designed by Holden and completed in 1929, it was then the tallest office building in London, an imposing cruciform 'Gotham city' tower of granite and Portland stone, decorated with sculptures by Eric Gill, Eric Aumonier, Alfred Horace, Henry Moore and Jacob Epstein. It was Epstein's contributions rather than the architecture that attracted controversy. In 1908 Epstein's nude stone figures for another Holden building – the British Medical Association on the Strand –

---

17   On his first afternoon at Oxford, Charles Ryder in Evelyn Waugh's novel *Brideshead Revisited* adorns his rooms with a poster by Edward McKnight Kauffer – Pick's principal poster artist.

had provoked vicious press notices. The BMA had stood by the statues but they were eventually chiselled off by the building's new owners, the Rhodesian High Commission in 1937. *Night* and *Day*, his two pieces for 55 Broadway, were branded obscene. *Day* was tarred and feathered and in the storm Pick offered his resignation. It was refused, the brouhaha subsided and the statues scarcely cause a blinked eyelid today. Epstein, sadly, did not receive another public commission for 20 years.

Pick worked himself exceptionally hard, putting in around 16 hours a day, six days a week, and he expected a comparable diligence from his staff. Fools were not suffered, gladly or otherwise. In stark contrast to Ashfield, who was an urbane charmer, as at ease with stationmen, flower girls and passengers as he was with politicians and shareholders, Pick, raised among devout Congregationalists in Lincolnshire, could be cold, intimidating and severe. Their differing personalities were, however, essentially complementary: Ashfield was the great door knocker, palm greaser (metaphorically) and Pick the dedicated administrator with a visionary eye, with a visionary zeal even, for good design. They would have made a perfect cop show duo.[18]

But it was with the arrival of the London Transport Passenger Board (London Transport) that Pick found the canvas to match his ambitions. Just as London Transport was structurally akin to the BBC, so Pick's ethos had always been fundamentally similar

---

18   Sunday nights ITV1 . . . *Ashfield and Pick: No Need to Ask a P'liceman*. Bill Nighy is Lord Stanley and Warren Clarke is Frank Pick in *Murder on the Metropolitan Line . . . The Piccadilly Palaver . . . The Arnos Grove Assassin . . .* 'Sorry, Mr Man Ray, we'll have to discuss this poster later, they've found another body at Dover Street.' All too believable, isn't it?

to that of the BBC's first general manager, John Reith – and social improvement was a key tenet in both the Presbyterian and the Quaker traditions that Reith, a son of the manse, and Pick were born into. A founding member of the Design and Industries Association, in 1932 Pick had mounted an exhibition of good British design in the booking hall of Embankment (then Charing Cross) Underground station. The 'goodness of a thing', in Pick's verdict, was in 'its fitness for use'. His belief that ordinary passengers, ordinary Londoners deserved the best, went far beyond supplying an excellent travelling service; it was about enriching and improving their lives by surrounding them with, in essence, simple, beautiful and well-made objects.

He embraced the challenge of melding a collection of bus, tube and tram companies into a cohesive whole with gusto, insisting that meticulous standards of uniform design were applied across the board; on new maps, posters, stations, buses, trains, fixtures and fittings, everything specifically created for the network. Seat fabrics were created by Paul Nash. The German graphic designer Hans Schleger was commissioned to convert Johnston's Underground roundel – itself now reworked into a new London Transport logo – into a symbol for request bus stops (another innovation – before their appearance passengers had been able to hail a bus at any point on its route). Holden created bus shelters, little Zen temples to travel, with spreading roofs, benches and compact litter boxes on their sides.

Pick left London Transport in 1940, but even after his death in 1941, he remained London Transport's conscience, its superego. The culture he'd established there, his insistence on excellence, became the binding principle of the entire organi-

zation. It was a principle that was central to the Routemaster's design.

Unlike Frank Pick, Charles Holden or Harry Beck, Albert Arthur Molteno Durrant is obscure to most Londoners. And yet, as the person who played a pivotal role in the design and maintenance of the city's buses from 1933 until his retirement in 1965, he made a considerable contribution to London life. Durrant was London Transport's longest serving chief officer and, in the true spirit of Pick's enterprise, did much to ensure that levels of continuity and standards of bus design were maintained after the war. Durrant was the real driving force behind the Routemaster.

An engineer's engineer, in photographs Durrant looks every inch the boffin. A neat, wiry man with a cranium like a ball-bearing and a pair of large oval Bakelite glasses fixed on the end of his nose, he gives the impression of someone happiest in a lab coat. Preferably one with a top pocket chock full of rulers, rubbers, pencils and fountain pens. To this day, those who knew him speak of him with the kind of reverence that flushed-faced men in tweeds adopt when conversations in snug bars turn to the topic of old headmasters, COs, Churchill. Thatcher, maybe. Heads nod respectfully, euphemisms abound ('He was a one, all right', 'Detail was his thing'), nicknames proliferate ('The Old Man', 'Bill','The Guv'nor'), and if the actual character of the subject in question becomes a tad oblique, the respect and admiration inspired are unmistakable.

Durrant joined the London General Omnibus Company in 1919, rising to the post of chief engineer shortly before London Transport was founded. At the General he'd been involved in the development of the first mass-produced diesel bus, the STL – subsequently adopted by London Transport as their main double decker.

In the 1930s, Durrant's stint as the chief engineer of London Transport's bus and coach division culminated in the creation of a flagship bus, the RT, in 1939. Embodying the principles of industrial design (fitness for purpose, modernity) that Pick insisted on, the RT set new heights in engineering, style and passenger comfort. Only 150 were built before the war stopped production in May 1940.

For many the RT bus, in its post-war incarnations, is *the* London Bus.

In the aftermath of the Dunkirk evacuation that June, the Tank Board acquired Durrant's services for the nation. Although, apparently, somewhat reluctant to leave his buses, he became the director of tank research and development at the government research centre at Chobham in Surrey. This did not prevent him on occasion from sneaking back to Chiswick, test vehicle in tow, to use the facilities there. The floor in Chiswick's experimental workshop is reported to have borne the scars of tank treadmarks until its dying days. However unorthodox Durrant's methods, the results of his stint at the Tank Board were, by anyone's standards, impressive. It arrived too late for the war, but his team devised the Centurion – the British Army's tank of choice for the next 20 years. In honour of his contribution to British tanking, the denizens of Chobham named a street, a *way* to be exact, after him.

With bus building on hold, Chiswick Works was turned over to aircraft production. In collaboration with other west London motor companies such as Park Royal Coachworks and Chrysler Motor Cars, it helped build around 700 Handley Page Halifax Bombers. Through this war work, LT engineers and designers came into contact with the latest innovations in aircraft manufacture, including the use of lighter metals like aluminium and construction from interchangeable component parts.

When peace came, Durrant and co gradually set about exploring how these techniques and materials could be applied to buses. To begin with the RT was completely redesigned to make bus building more a process of assembly than manufacture. This greatly improved efficiency. Buses were not only easier and faster to build but they also required a less skilled workforce to build and maintain them, which saved on training and, overall, on labour costs.

The first batch of these new RT buses with their gleaming paint-work and lavish interiors hit the drab London streets in 1947, just as Clement Attlee's Labour government was forced to bring in a series of austerity measures to stall an economic crisis and London Transport was itself passing into national ownership under the British Transport Commission.

Grim as life could be – and with milk allowances reduced to two pints a week, newspapers slimmed to four pages, and pota-toes and bread joining the list of rationed comestibles, it wasn't much fun[19] – this was a period of optimism, a period of bold schemes and initiatives: the NHS, the Welfare State, New Towns, the Edinburgh Festival. A time when people really did believe that things could only get better, even if that was only because nobody wanted things to get any worse.

London Transport was no different; like the nation it was look-ing to the future. Pre-war plans to scrap the last remaining trams were reactivated and it was decided that new RT-type diesel buses would replace them. Memos about what might, in turn, replace the RT were already circulating in the spring of 1947 – only a few months after the RT diesels had entered passenger service. There was nothing particularly unusual about this; London Transport engineers continually looked ahead to the 'next' bus, and new ideas and lessons learnt in operation were continually fed into new prototypes.

It would, however, take another four years of research work,

---

19 London Transport's staff magazine kindly gave tips on how stale bread could be revitalized: 'Put a saucer of hot water on the bottom shelf of a moderately hot oven, place the loaf on the shelf above and leave for 20 minutes.'

trials, discussions with manufacturers and men from various ministries, interminable committee meetings, reports, time and motion studies, countless cups of urn-stewed tea, and a change of government, before a course toward the Routemaster was finally plotted; and a further three years until the prototype was complete; and another four years after that before the bus entered production. Sputnik took less time to get into space.[20]

---

20 In February 1951, as some indication of the meticulousness of its working methods, London Transport demonstrated the prototype of a new ticketing machine invented by Mr George Gibson, a former superintendent at the Stockwell punch works. It dispensed with pre-printed tickets, printing directly on to a blank roll, and could supply 300 tickets on each roll. Gibson had devoted over seven years to perfecting it. 'For Mr Gibson,' *London Transport Magazine* chirped, 'this invention is the climax of his life's work . . . by trade a watchmaker, he came to London from his native village of Duns, in the border country to join the LGOC . . . Using the new machine,' the magazine continued, 'a conductor issues a ticket, including giving change where necessary, in an average time of 5.11 seconds. With the old-time ticket rack and punch it takes 6.15 seconds.'

4

THE BUS OF THE FUTURE

Durrant, as he recorded in 1956, kicked off that long and winding journey with a bit of what would now be called blue skies thinking. He began by asking the operating managers 'to try to erase from their minds all the past features they had specified, to think out their requirements from the rock bottom . . . the aim being to get down to the ideal bus from their point of view.' Their notion of an ideal bus, as it turned out, happened to be remarkably similar to what had gone before, as an LT press release about the Routemaster issued in March 1958 hints: 'Operational research showed that the orthodox position of many features was in fact the best place for them.' Dr Pangloss couldn't have put it any better.

After substantial and lengthy deliberations about larger single-decker buses, bigger double-decker buses with doors, double-decker buses with rear engines, double-decker buses with doors in the middle and underfloor-engined double deckers, what the operators decided they wanted was a new front-engined, rear-staircased, rear-open-platformed double decker. If this was orthodox, verging on the stolidly conservative, Durrant's department would ensure its construction was entirely radical – as in many aspects of its engineering it still is.

Buses, traditionally, have tended to have a body and a chassis, with two separate manufacturers producing each part in a never the twain, we-do-the-body, they-do-the-chassis kind of way; both sides meeting infrequently and, like hamsters, purely to mate and bring a new bus into being. From the outset, reducing weight was uppermost in everybody's mind at London Transport; a lighter bus could carry a greater number of passengers and be more fuel-efficient. To achieve this, a chassis-less construction was advocated. The body would be reinforced so that it could carry the gearbox and the engine, thus dispensing with the need for a standard chassis; and, bingo, bringing the weight down. This mode of integral construction, called monocoque, was fairly common on cars of the day. Morris Minors, for example, were monocoques, and some trolleybuses in the late 1930s had been built along these lines, but this was serious stuff for a British diesel bus.

Bus bodies had been constructed of aluminium (and duralumin) in the 1920s, but steel and timber were the most common materials for buses in the 1940s and well on into the 50s. Drawing on their experiences of aircraft production, London Transport engineers believed that alloys could be used which would be lighter and just as durable.

In 1949, the bus division had also acquired a site at Aldenham in Hertfordshire to build a dedicated overhaul works. Chiswick was by now struggling to cope with a fleet that, once tram replacement was complete, was expected to exceed 8000. Originally kitted out as a tube depot for the Northern Line in the late 30s, Aldenham, like Chiswick, had spent the war on aircraft work, overhauling Handley Page Bombers. Now it found itself surplus to the Underground's requirements. The adoption of Abercrombie's Greater London Plan (1944) after the war had effectively kyboshed longstanding schemes to extend the Edgware branch to Bushey, since all the land around it now fell within the Green Belt.[21] A new, bespoke overhaul works offered the prospect of even greater possibilities for assembly line-style components, which would be easier and cheaper to fashion in alloys.

What was becoming increasingly apparent to all at London Transport was that 'the private motor car' posed an unavoidable and, perhaps, insurmountable threat to their services. Even before discussions about any new London buses had begun, the effects of the car on the capital were being noted. In May 1947, it was announced that parking restrictions – yellow lines – would be introduced on some central roads, and a traffic jam near King's Cross station that June received full coverage in the *Evening Standard*. The following year, LT launched its own 'Shop between 10 and 4', 'Avoid the Rush Hour' advertising campaign. Durrant –

---

21   Tube enthusiasts are wont to describe this decision as a calamity, a missed
     opportunity on a par with the failure of Wren's Great Fire rebuilding plan. The
     names of the stations unbuilt – Brockley Hill, Elstree South and Bushey
     Heath – fall from their lips like the liturgy. 'Think of it,' one ex-LT staffer I met
     at the Acton Depot museum said without a trace of irony, 'Elstree South.'

in particular – felt that any new bus for London would have to match, surpass even, the levels of comfort found in your average Morris or Austin to compete.

Having already opted to scrap the capital's lingering trams,[22] London Transport was faced with the thorny issue of what it should do about its 1760 electric trolleybuses. With no rails to guide them, they were more free to move about the road than trams, but they were still widely regarded as obstructive to traffic. All the trolleybuses on a single route, say the 611 to Highgate Village, would share the same stretch of wire. Rather like beads on an abacus, they travelled in series, and couldn't overtake one another. Unlike a row of buses – where an empty (or emptier) bus can race on ahead to the next stop, spreading the distribution of passengers – one full trolleybus could easily block up an entire route, as each subsequent bus bunched up behind it. This made them unpopular with motorists and passengers alike.

Their frequent appearances in John Betjeman's wistful output in the late 40s and early 50s, in poems such as *Harrow-on-the-Hill* ('And the constant click and kissing of the trolleybuses hissing') and *St Saviour's Aberdeen Park, Highbury, London N* ('Stop the trolleybus, stop! . . . Of weariest worn-out London') serves only to nail them as a faintly anachronistic species.

The decision to scrap the trolleybuses wasn't made public until April 1954. But as early as 1951 Durrant's new alloy double-decker bus was already being whispered of as a possible successor to the RT *and* the trolleybus. (The subsequent design was made

---

22   The last London tram ran on 5 July 1952.

baggy enough to allow an electric-powered version, should – and it was a big *should* as far as most London Transport executives were concerned – it be required. Unless you were a dodgem car this was not a good time to be an electric vehicle.) To many this was a monstrous wrong turn in London Transport policy; and with the benefit of hindsight, they were right. Pollution-free and virtually silent, the trolleybuses were a safe and environmentally sound means of transport.[23] But with rising car ownership, they were seen to be as relevant to the modern metropolis as the horse bus.

By early 1952, a 13-point outline was laid down. From now on all roads would lead to Routemaster. The vehicle, known for the moment as IM, would be a double-decker bus of 'chassis-less type and of integral metal construction and light alloys'. It would be 8 ft wide and 27 ft long, and 14 ft 4½ in high. A target of 11½ tons was set for its weight. The new bus would be a collaborative effort. AEC on Windmill Lane in Southall and Park Royal beside the Regent's Canal would work with London Transport on the prototype. AEC would contribute to the engineering and running equipment, and Park Royal would fashion the bodywork.

As noted earlier, Associated Equipment Ltd (AEC) had been formed as a subsidiary chassis-building company when London General took over Vanguard in 1909, and later formed part of the Underground Group. It grew to become a significant bus and truck manufacturer in its own right, and Britain's major exporter of commercial and public service vehicles. When the London

---

23 After some 33 years' absence, trolleybuses made a comeback to the streets of Rome in 2004.

Passenger Board came into being in 1933, it was agreed that London Transport could continue to place about 70 per cent of its business with AEC, while the other 30 per cent was put out to tender with other manufacturers. If AEC was unable to meet LT's needs for any reason, LT was free to shop elsewhere. (In accordance with this deal, two of the four prototype Routemasters were equipped by Leyland, and, to keep AEC on their toes, between 1962 and 1964 close to 600 Routemasters were fitted with Leyland engines.)

This arrangement worked very well for London Transport and AEC. As near west London neighbours, their engineers met frequently, pooled ideas and swapped experimental data. AEC engines powered more than 4000 London Transport RT buses, and the slogan 'Builder of London's Buses' was one the company cherished with no small degree of pride. (Leyland, who had supplied a number of buses for London Transport over the years, could only muster the faintly submissive 'Leyland serves London', though it was the dominant bus producer in the provinces.)

Park Royal Vehicles (a sibling of AEC since it was purchased by their umbrella company, Associated Commercial Vehicles in 1949) also enjoyed a strong historical relationship with London Transport, having supplied bodies for fleets of STL double deckers in the 1930s and far more than 3000 RTs.

With the building plan in place and AEC and Park Royal on board, the next stage was to formulate what the new bus should look like. To aid this process London Transport engaged one of Britain's few industrial design consultants, Douglas Scott.

5

SUNG YELLOW AND CHINESE GREEN

'I shall never forget how I got paid for the Routemaster job,' Douglas Scott informed James Woudhuysen in *Design* magazine in October 1983. 'The money,' he added with, I like to imagine, probably a sliver of a pause, 'came from petty cash.' There's something very British about the story. You can picture the tin box and key, chitties signed and countersigned, the mottled notes and coins handed over in a brown envelope, waxy to the touch; the whole, mildly embarrassing transaction accompanied by the odd cough or a clearing of a throat. No fuss, mind; everyone just getting on with the task in hand.

If ever there was a product designer whose work could be characterized by its understated good manners, it's Scott. From his Potterton boiler and his redesign of the Aga (a restyling in 1938 that stood the cooker in good stead for the next 40 years),

to his GPO call box K8 and his Rediffusion radio sets, his designs
are models of practical, restrained style. Form never oversteps
function; as distinctly British as toast and marmalade, ELO and
the novels of Anthony Powell.

Scott himself would never be entirely happy with the finished
Routemaster; late modifications to the bonnet to accommodate
the powered steering unit, in particular, distressed him. He died
in 1990, when his rich burgundy and yellow tartan moquette seat
covers remained – pretty much – standard, and so at least he was
spared the sight of a range of interior fabrics unveiled in 1992
that appeared expressly designed to pacify e-upped clubbers in
need of a last fractal hit on the N38 home.[24]

Born in 1913 in Kennington, south London, Scott trained as a
silversmith at the Central School of Arts and Crafts and began his
professional career designing neo-classical and art-deco light fittings. In 1936 at a point when, as he confessed to his biographer
Jonathan Glancey, if he designed another light fitting he'd
'develop an attack of the screaming abdabs', Scott secured a position in the London office of the industrial designers Raymond
Loewy Associates. Raymond Loewy, a debonair (harsher voices
might say flashy) Paris-born American with an immaculately
trimmed pencil moustache, was the pioneer of 'clean-lined'
design or streamlining. Inspired by aircraft styling, he brought
flowing parabolas to railway locomotives, ocean liners and

---

24 There was, incidentally, a techno record label called Routemaster Records
    which released such endearing floorshakers as Immersion and Dirtball's 'I Have
    to Take My Knickers Off' and 'Fuk It, I'm a Drug Bucket' and whose logo was
    a cartoon of a Routemaster bus cutting it up on the decks.

ordinary commercial household objects and appliances, producing ovoid pencil sharpeners and rounded radio cabinets that in their uncluttered simplicity Loewy felt answered 'a subconscious yearning for the polished essential'. Dimestore Freud maybe, but it was during his stint at Loewy's that Scott mastered the undulating curve, a recurring leitmotiv in his *oeuvre* – as the exterior he devised for the Routemaster attests. While Scott toiled on the Routemaster, on the other side of the Atlantic his ex-boss was refining the Greyhound Scenicruiser bus, the classic crenellated aluminium bullet that beatnik odysseys were made for.[25]

The Routemaster was not Scott's first bus. In 1948 he received a commission from London Transport to design the bodywork and interiors for three versions of a new single decker – the AEC chassised Regal Four (RF, to the perennially acronym-minded souls at LT and AEC). The earliest models of the RF – dapper, lozenge-shaped coaches with a red and cream livery (imagine, and I'm positing this as a good thing, a Topic chocolate bar on four wheels) – ferried visitors around the Festival of Britain on the South Bank in 1951. On the strength of the RF, London Transport approached Scott again early the following year about styling the Routemaster.

Scott's position at London Transport was always somewhat precarious. There were, he remembered, 'no established procedures for dealing with consultant designers, who in those days were still regarded as rather strange people'. The precise

---

25 Loewy, ever the brilliant reductivist when it came to logos – his revised Shell logo was . . . well, still a shell, but *my* what a shell – was also responsible for Greyhound's leaping dog insignia.

dimensions of the bus, following negotiations with the Metropolitan Police Carriage Office, had already been set, so there were very clear limits on what he could do with its exterior. Scott at first envisaged the bus having a full-frontal cab; his RF had a full-frontal cab, and bus and coach design generally was moving in that direction. His preliminary sketches, however, were almost instantaneously vetoed by union representatives who felt that such a design would make the bus trickier for their members to drive. London Transport also expressed concerns about driver visibility, and Scott was duly instructed to supply plans with a traditional half-cab and bonnet, which in the final bus one cannot help but anthropomorphize into a nose.

Durrant's prevailing stipulation was that the bus must be an attractive piece of street furniture (a phrase favoured, incidentally, by Frank Pick) and as such it had to fit into some recognized

London norms – an unofficial London Transport bus motto was 'evolution not revolution'. Lumbered, as he saw it, with 'long, box dimensions', Scott was anxious to avoid something like a shoe-box, and began (as he told Glancey) to 'steal the shape, pinching half an inch here, three-quarters of an inch there'. The curvaceous body he eventually arrived at was not only enormously pleasing on the eye but it was also later found to have distinct advantages when it came to cleaning. The sparge of London Transport's new bus washing machines travelled evenly over the top of its roof; when boxier models came into being in the 60s and 70s, it was discovered that the sparge actually jumped when it hit a straight edge, leaving a dirty mark.

Where Scott took his design cues from can really only be a matter of speculation – those in the know mutter darkly about a '99 country bus', but to the untrained eye more obvious candidates from London street life present themselves: the RT and trolleybuses of the day. Scott's first mock-up was, in fact, deemed too similar to a trolleybus by London Transport's chairman, and a series of amendments was made before the prototype RM1 came into being. In trials this in turn was pronounced 'a disaster' by one senior engineer and Scott undertook further revisions to the bonnet and grille, returning again in 1955 and in 1956 to work on the bodywork of later prototypes and the final produc-tion models – which were always a disappointment to him.

The Routemaster, it's worth remembering, was a collabora-tive piece. Scott and Durrant's chief engineer, Eric Ottoway, clashed frequently over the bodywork design. Its unorthodox construction called for some ingenious engineering; rather like a screwdriver with adjustable heads, or a set of Meccano, each part of the bus was tooled to be completely interchangeable. Such engineering concerns occasionally compromised some of Scott's ideas for the bus, but the end result was an extraordinarily flexible vehicle: Of the four main variants built in its lifespan, two were rejigged with little fuss to offer front entrances. And when London Transport in 1961 decided to increase the number of passengers the bus could carry, it simply dropped an additional 2 ft 6 in panel into the centre of the body. The extra length allowed another row of seats to be fitted to each deck, upping the capacity from 64 to 72. (These longer buses were known as RML Routemasters.)

With the interiors, Scott had a far freer hand. Durrant believed that they had to be as luxurious as possible if they were to stand any chance of tempting people from their cars, and Scott delivered interiors that were almost worthy of a Bentley. Even 15 years ago or so to travel on a Routemaster with the remnants of its original décor intact felt like being conveyed about the city in the lounge of an illustrious, if by now gone-to-seed, club. In the smoky fug of the upper deck, you half expected (or wished) the conductor to dispense port and cigars as they collected the fares.

Scott's final colour scheme was a triumph of style and durability. 'Burgundy lining panels, Chinese green window surrounds, and Sung yellow ceilings', as the official description had it. Chinese green was a tad fanciful (slate-green or grey would be more accurate) but, dubious Orientalism aside, the Sung yellow ceilings proved a particular boon – they not only brightened the interior of the bus, they also camouflaged the nicotine stains that bloomed on the top deck. Repainting was required only every

seven years. A survey carried out by British Leyland in 1984 found that 40 per cent of buses in service had their original interior paint finish, which could be revived with nothing more than car polish.

In the late 1940s, in what for him was a rare entry into luxury goods, Scott had designed a set of matching luggage cases – the Pendragon range – with a check finish and tartan interiors. (They were displayed as a part of the Design Review at the Festival of Britain.) For the Routemaster, Scott created his own tartan moquette of dark red and yellow. The check gave the bus an added chic and was also enormously practical. The dominant dark red hid dirt; the yellow stripes complemented the ceilings and lightened the overall tone of the fabric. The cloth proved remarkably hardwearing and there are many stories of busmen using it to carpet their hallways and cover their settees.

Initially, Scott wanted to use solid fibreglass frames for the seats and handrails but these were found to be heavier than tubular metal and wood. A lot of thought went into the seats themselves. A bench shape with a full back was specifically chosen to thwart pickpockets, who might have used any gaps to pilfer from their fellow passengers. The seats were then edged with leather, classy and yet entirely functional, because it helped passengers to slide in and out of their seats using the handrail. The smooth edge also helped reduce wear and tear on the conductors' trousers (or snags on stockings, presumably, not that this appeared to have occurred to anyone at the time) as they patrolled up and down the aisle of the bus. The seats were fixed to inner stress panels, so if the bus was hit, it was only the outer body shell that got damaged. The cushions were designed to drop in on spigots. If a cushion got soiled or vandalized (perish the thought in 1954) it could be

changed in a matter of minutes. As for lighting, Scott had considered fluorescent tubes but they were turned down on grounds of expense and because it was felt that bulbs would be easier and quicker for bus crews to replace.

It was Scott who refined the cubbyhole under the stairs for the conductor, a sanctuary where a brief *pas de deux* could be performed with the passengers to facilitate entrances and exits. Such careful attention to detail was continued by London Transport's own designers in the driver's cab, where the handbrake lever was shifted to the left to assist access and, as on the RT-types, a sliding rather than hinged door was installed to prevent any accidents with passing vehicles or pedestrians. On warmer days, the driver could travel with the door open; a distinct boon in a world of work where air conditioning had yet to happen. For passengers, there were quarter-drop wind-down windows for extra ventilation; most provincial buses in the 1950s were fitted with sliding top windows, which tended to rattle when the bus was moving and looked cheap. London's RTs had half-drop windows but these were prone to jamming and falling open unexpectedly. The Routemaster was, therefore, windowed to provide draughts only when they were needed and not to rattle.

Heating systems continued to be a rarity on all but the more expensive private cars but Durrant had insisted that saloon heating should be included. LT's single-decker RF buses had heating of a sort and in cold snaps 55 Broadway was inundated with angry letters demanding to know why their double deckers weren't heated. The system eventually devised for the Routemaster aped that then found on private cars. As the bus was in

motion fresh air was drawn in through grilles below the destination board at the front. The air passed over a heating radiator, and
a diffuser then fed the heat around the bus. When the heat was
turned off, cool air could be eddied through the bus in the same
way to ventilate it. That was the theory, anyhow.

As well as lacking heating, the RTs could give rather a bumpy
ride. They had pre-selective gearboxes. To change up the driver
was supposed to take his foot off the accelerator, engage the gear
pedal (the equivalent of the clutch) and then reapply the accelerator. There's an unavoidable jerkiness about this transmission:
a case of brrum, brrum, clunk, whirr, and then back to brrum,
brrum. 'It's not,' as one ex-driver put it, 'an easy bus to drive
smooth.' Passengers moving down the aisles had unnerving and
jarring experiences at times.

To improve standards of passenger comfort and to make the
bus simpler to drive, a fully automatic gearbox, where the driver
could change gear even with the accelerator down, was devised
for the Routemaster. That trolleybus drivers weren't used to vehicles with gears was a further, and by no means negligible
consideration. Trolleybus replacement would be able to proceed
with less staff wastage if the new bus presented as few challenges
as possible. The gear selector pedal was therefore eliminated
entirely, and the gears, operating on an electro-hydraulic system,
were controlled by a simple lever on the steering column. Power
assisted steering was included on the production models. Its sheer
ease to drive made it known as 'the driver's bus' among many of
the crews.

*

Another improvement to give 'greater softness and more comfortable riding conditions', decided upon and mapped out in the 13-point plan, was the use of independent front suspension on the Routemasters. Again, this was common on cars – those bouncing bathtub Minors, Populars, Westminsters and Oxfords – but groundbreaking for a bus. All double deckers were required by law to pass a 'tilt test' to check their stability – to ensure, for example, that they didn't topple over when Class 3B from St Custards swarmed *en masse* to the top deck and started playing rock-a-bye baby. The minimum requirement was that a bus should be able to tilt 28 degrees from the vertical without capsizing. In early trials, the Routemaster showed that it could tilt far in excess of 30°, making it one of the most stable double deckers ever built. 'We thought it was never going over,' Roy Gentile, a draughtsman who worked on the Routemaster, remembered in 1992. 'It went beyond our wildest dreams.' The front and rear axles had coil springs. If you watch a Routemaster edging through traffic, you'll see that the nose of the bus bobs from side to side, ever so slightly, as if in greeting, due to the sensitivity of its suspension. It's also what makes hopping on and off at the back such a pleasure, because the springs supply that little give, that *al dente* moment, as your feet touch the platform.

One other and quite startling technical innovation was its power hydraulic brakes. Hydraulic brakes were invented back in 1918 and fitted to Chrysler cars in the 1920s and the Morris Minor in 1934. They work on a simple pressure principle: the force of your leg on the brake pedal generates hydraulic pressure in a master cylinder, which then pumps fluid through the lines and hoses to cylinders and callipers on the wheels, forcing the brake shoes against the drums. They are very responsive and continue to be standard on cars but usually offer less braking power than air-brakes so were not generally used on buses and trucks.

The RTs were fitted with a type of compressed airbrake but there were problems with losses in pressure. Their valves were liable to clog up with dirt, and in icy conditions any excess moisture froze and disabled them entirely. In 1947, when discussions about new buses for London were in their infancy, cold weather was a more pressing concern. Britain had just experienced one of the coldest winters on record, and what remains the snowiest of them. Temperatures in London that February dropped to minus 9 degrees Fahrenheit. By chance, later that year Lockheed offered London Transport a hydraulic braking system that it had created for aircraft. It ran on mineral oil, which does not freeze or corrode, and, as the oil was kept flowing continuously through the accumulators, a constant pressure level could be maintained and brake failure eliminated.

6

TOO TRAD, DAD

By August 1954, seven years of murmurs, memos, arguments, working parties, sketches, mock-ups, and preliminary tests and trials were slowly approaching a conclusion. The prototype was ready, or at least ready to face the world. For British bus and truck manufacturers in the 1950s, there was only one place to launch a new vehicle: the annual Commercial Motor Show at Earl's Court.

That year's show, the seventeenth, opened on the 24 September and there, among 'a handsome' 5-cwt Ford Thames van, and 'a versatile' Morris Dormobile Junior, stood the newly named 'London Transport Routemaster'. The *London Illustrated News* noted that it was 'built on revolutionary lines to carry eight more people than the present London bus but which weighs less'.

The name 'Routemaster' and the type code RM[26] weren't made public until 13 September – just 11 days prior to the show. With the exception of the codes IM and, later on, RT12,[27] no name is recorded, or was it seems seriously considered, before the beginning of September. At that point, Durrant suggested 'Roadmaster' but this, reputedly, was thought too bullying.

Names, even of buses, are subject to the whims of fashion. 'Masters' were in vogue that season: a Rowe Hillmaster truck was another new vehicle at Earl's Court, while cinema-goers that year watched an apartment-bound Jimmy Stewart trim his stubble with a Sunbeam Shavemaster in Alfred Hitchcock's *Rear Window*. The choice of the prefix 'Route' – perfectly apt since buses do run on routes – did nonetheless lend a certain transatlantic edge to it. Londoners in 1954 were teetering on the brink of the Rock 'n' Roll era. The younger among them would have known 'Route 66 (Get Your Kicks On)' from Nat King Cole's 1946 recording. The word would have been as capable of conjuring up images of the desert highways of Flagstaff, Arizona, as of the number 11 to Walham Green. When other British double-decker buses of that age were called 'Titan', 'Regent' and 'Lodekka'[28] not everyone thought Routemaster an entirely appropriate name for a bus destined for Knightsbridge, Bond Street and Royal Kensington.

---

26   These type letters,' said the LT press release, 'will not only be descriptive of the
       name given to the model but will also perpetuate the letter "R" which has been
       associated with London Tranport's post-war vehicle of standard design (ie RT,
       RTL, RTW, RLH, RF and RFW).'
27   Wasn't he in *Star Wars*?
28   A suitably ugly Soviet-esque name for a very ugly bus. The Lodekka was a
       Behemoth with a radiator like the mouth of a plankton-guzzling whale, and it's
       a terrible pun, ie low decker. Personally, I can't help feeling it was a shame that

The name wasn't alone in meeting an initially cool reception. The new bus's engineering and innovative construction were widely praised – *Bus & Coach* magazine said it was technically the most interesting exhibit of the show – but the overwhelming reaction at Earl's Court was that 'London's Bus of the Future' (as it was billed) was, well, a tad trad, Dad. Downright old-fashioned, actually. 'It looks,' opined the trade journal *Motor Transport*, 'to be just another London bus . . . a little larger and more modern in appearance, but nothing more.' The future in 1954 was more . . . shall we say futuristic. The Festival of Britain had blazed a trail for modernism in London within its space age Skylon, a 300 ft tall aluminium and steel sculpture on the South Bank. But with atomic tests at Bikini in full swing and the *Daily Mail* that July confidently predicting that 'there will be flying saucer landings in England next year',[29] any claims to modernity came with certain obligations, expectations. To be modern was very modern, and it meant being strikingly different from the past. Placed beside the prototype of Leyland's Lowloader – a novel rear-engined bus previewed that September – the Routemaster, for all its interchangeable aluminium, aircraft brakes and coil springs, was too familiar, too cosy, a wheel or two stuck in yesteryear. Not *now*

---

bus names didn't mirror the popular personal names of the day, the London Transport Maurice, Colin or Douglas would have been nice. On a related note, just think how much more devastating to Nazi morale, the Spitfires or Hurricanes would have been, if they had been called Alan or Geoffrey.

29   The piece, which appeared on 8 July 1954, was written by the 'West End Stage Star' Agnes Bernelle, whose husband, the composer Desmond Leslie, was the co-author of the book *Flying Saucers Have Landed*. A flying saucer song even made its way into the musical *Salad Days*, which had recently opened in the West End.

enough for then. Which, in part, explains its longevity; free of 50s gimmicks, its design has weathered far better than that of any of its contemporaries.

At the time, its superficial resemblance to its predecessor provoked a number of unfavourable comparisons. One of the most vitriolic early reviews appeared, perhaps surprisingly, in *Buses Illustrated*, then hailed as 'the only periodical for bus enthusiasts'. Home to 'Reminiscing' columnist 'Bob Ticket' ('I would like to give you some of my impressions of transport during the period 1924–1939, particularly in my native city of Manchester . . .') and with regular features on the likes of Mrs Gertrude Leather and her Bus Riders' Club, a society for women 'who prefer', as their writer saw it, 'to sit behind a throbbing Gardner than to stand over a hot stove',[30] this organ of the amateur, in the noblest sense

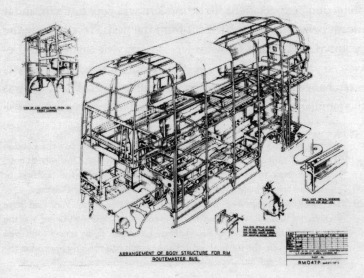

ARRANGEMENT OF BODY STRUCTURE FOR RM
ROUTEMASTER BUS.

of the word, made for an unlikely assassin. But bus enthusiasts are nothing if not enthusiastic. Like all lovers their passions run high, and any inadequacies in their objects of desire are taken as affronts to their own taste and integrity. The Routemaster, in their eyes, was an unworthy usurper, impudent pipsqueak and wicked stepmother rolled into one. If the RT had had boots, the Routemaster would not, you suspect in their judgement, have been fit to lick them, let alone tie their straps.

RM1 was 'a fascinating study', their anonymous reviewer admitted. They conceded that the designers deserved credit for not allowing standards of comfort or interior finish to suffer in cutting weight. '. . . indeed the interior of the RM has all the neatness of the RT allied to a cheerfulness which seems likely to be equally effective in summer and winter . . . From the rear, the RM is considerably more shapely than the standard RT . . . Otherwise,' and here came the killer blow, 'the design generally fails to reach the RT standards, still less show *any* improvement on it.' My italics, but *ouch*.

---

30   A Gardner, in case you were wondering, was a common bus engine.

7

A ROBIN IN THE SNOW

The show and critical mauling over, RM1 went back home to Chiswick. There its engineers and designers absorbed the criticism, sighed, shrugged, chewed on the ends of their pencils for a minute maybe two, made a mental note to cancel their subscriptions to *Buses Illustrated* as they lodged the moistened 2Hs back behind their ears, and then rolled up their sleeves and got on with the serious business of preparing 'the old girl' for the road. By February 1955, as tinkering on RM1 continued, they'd already finished a second prototype, RM2, and over the next two years built two more prototypes (RML3 and CRL4, a coach version with a rear door for Greenline travel), both engined by Leyland but with bodies from Weymann and Eastern Coach Works, respectively.

Before any of the prototypes could come within a yard of a paying passenger they were subjected to what can really only be described as gruelling test programmes. RM1, for example, was taken to Durrant's old war-time haunt, the Fighting Vehicle Proving Ground at Chobham, and also to the Motor Industry Research Association Testing Ground at Nuneaton, clocking up more than 6000 miles in conditions devised to mimic the very worst it could face on the road, including 'a full-lock skid at 30 mph'.

Extraordinary as it might seem to us now, in our risk-averse and liability-sensitive age, the one test none of the prototypes underwent prior to service was a full-on smash. Engineers at Chiswick toyed with the idea of driving one of the prototypes at a wall but baulked at the cost. (Volunteer drivers were, a reliable source has informed me, thin on the ground.) In the end, serendipity contrived that the third prototype, RML3, met a gravel lorry on the Edgware Road during passenger trials. Although its cab was severely damaged, the driver emerged unharmed. The gravel lorry, on the other hand, was written off.

The arrival of a new London bus was an event of national, and international, importance in the 1950s and the Routemaster's debut in the capital was heralded, quite naturally, with a short notice in *The Times* on Wednesday, 1 February 1956. 'The proto-type of a new London bus, the 64-passenger Routemaster will,' it stated, 'go into public service next Wednesday on Route 2 between Golders Green and Crystal Palace.[31] Production in quantity will start in 1958.'

---

31   The route had been chosen because it was one of the longest and crossed the heart of the city. London's shortest bus route was the 137a which ran from Sloane Square across Chelsea Bridge to the Pleasure Gardens, a distance of

February 1956 was one of coldest months London had suffered since 1947, and the morning of the Routemaster's maiden voyage was particularly frosty. It left Cricklewood Garage and made for Golders Green station, where it collected its first passengers, who were perhaps unaware of their cameo role in Routemaster history. As it drove through Child's Hill, Swiss Cottage and St John's Wood, the flurries of snow grew thicker. I like to think that with its shiny new paintwork, the bus forged on through the snow like a Christmas card robin – down to Baker Street, past Marble Arch, around Hyde Park Corner, and then to Victoria. Here it paused, exchanged the majority of its passengers, and then tumbled across Vauxhall Bridge for the shabby-genteel suburbs of south London: Vauxhall, Stockwell, Brixton, Herne Hill, Tulse Hill and West Norwood. Finally it reached the snow-capped hills of Crystal Palace. Then, of course, it had to turn around and go back again, but such is the Sisyphean lot of buses.

This cosy picture is dented by one less cosy fact: that day the RM1's much-vaunted heating system refused to be coaxed into life. Nonetheless, the bus remained in service until that August. In July, it was the star attraction of London's Bus Week, a series of celebrations concluding in a parade through Hyde Park to mark the centenary of the London General Omnibus Company. To monitor customer satisfaction, signs requesting comments were posted inside the bus. Its erratic heating system and the seats,

---

1½ miles. It was inaugurated in 1951 to help convey Festival of Britain visitors to the funfair in Battersea Park.

which had been filled with foam to save weight, attracted the bulk of the complaints. On the whole, though, the public liked it. They didn't love it yet but, given time, a few dates, a trip to the Rialto and a bag of chips with a pickled egg thrown in, and who knows, they might be willing to be seduced.

The scribes at *Buses Illustrated* certainly were. Now that they'd had a chance to see RM1 on the streets, hop on and take a ride, their attitudes softened considerably. 'The suspension of the Routemaster is without doubt, its most striking feature,' they piped. 'To get a fair comparison we rode immediately afterwards on a standard RT.' (Did they run for that second 'control' bus, notepads clasped in hand, satchels gently slapping their backsides as they dashed along, terrified that with every passing second the memory would ebb away to impair their critical judgements? I do like to imagine so.) 'On the RM we could feel few road irregularities, and the ride might be likened to that given by a good large modern private car, and not a commercial vehicle.' They were not entirely convinced by the gearbox and the engine which they found 'rather noisy' but 'generally' they 'liked the Routemaster very much'.

That summer, RM1 became every young boy's pin-up, or more accurately, scrapbook star; kids in the mid-1950s were not encouraged to adorn their bedroom walls with whatever the hell they liked. It appeared in the *Eagle* comic on 22 June. The *Eagle*'s mainstay was, of course, Dan Dare, an intergalactic Biggles who strove to thwart the evil ambitions of the Mekon, a malevolent dome-headed and green-skinned Venusian.[32] The Dan Dare strip

---

32 British comics, less fixated on communism than their American counterparts,

The Routemaster in the *Eagle* comic in 1956.

was set in the not-too-distant but technologically glitzy future, 1996; a time, or so its creators envisioned, when thanks to nuclear power electricity would be 'too cheap to meter', even if hairstyles continued to require a financially draining outlay in Brylcreem.

There was always a strong pedagogical element to the *Eagle*, with quizzes, diagrams and 'spotter' columns running alongside the main cartoon strips. These features were enormously popular with its readership during its 1950s heyday – at its peak the *Eagle*'s circulation nudged close to a million. Predominantly chaps on the cusp of adolescence (the teenager had scarcely been invented), its audience was possibly more technically literate and more interested in discovering how things worked than any generation that had gone before. In this pre-pop age, train- and bus-spotting for boys was the norm, and not a minority hobby which had the faint whiff of a medically recognized syndrome

evidently felt at liberty to choose a planet other than Mars – the Red Planet – as a source of possible danger.

about it. Ian Allen, a former railway clerk turned patron saint of spotting and the publisher of *Buses Illustrated*, had produced the first *ABC of London Transport* in 1948; a charming, if inaccurate, woodcut of RT567 by A N Wolstenholme on its front cover – the windows are wrong, apparently – and a slew of fleet numbers for the young (and not so young) enthusiast to seek out inside. For lads like Gerry Zierler, later to swap bus numbers for chart positions as a pirate radio DJ,[33] who grew up in Woodford in the 1950s, and avidly pursued the prototype Routemasters ('CRL4 was my passion,' he confessed), bus-spotting was 'endemic' at school. Competition over collecting fleet numbers was fierce and issues of *Buses Illustrated* were lovingly poured over. And so the *Eagle* featured 'London's Bus of the Future' as a centre-page spread spot, a cutaway colour drawing providing a detailed survey of all its workings. Wizzo.

The official verdict back at London Transport, however, was that those workings weren't working quite as tidily as they'd hoped. Active service had revealed a number of shortcomings in the design. The front end, especially, had caused Cricklewood drivers and Chiswick engineers to take the Lord's name in vain. As the bus had been shuttling back and forth from Golders Green to Crystal Palace, it had become painfully obvious that the fascia didn't allow enough ventilation to get to the brakes. In a relatively short space of time they overheated, a situation that had potentially lethal consequences if left unchecked. Scott and Ottoway and his team needed to create a new front for the bus.

The radiator, which was fitted under the engine, was a further

---

33   Radio 270's 'Wise' Guy Hamilton.

concern. Lying near to the road, in poor weather conditions it
quickly silted up. When RM1 re-emerged in November for the
Lord Mayor's parade – a muted affair because of the Suez crisis –
it sported a larger AEC engine and a new front with a radiator
and a grille; a look which, although continually refined over the
subsequent two years, as the bus went from four prototypes to a
finished production vehicle, is instantly recognizable as the
Routemaster we know. The bus we would love had arrived.

Turn again, Routemaster: a parade at the Lord Mayor's show
in November 1956.

8

TALK OF THE TOWN

On New Year's Eve 1956 at the New Lindsay Theatre Club in Notting Hill Gate a modest audience of revellers gathered to watch two men on a bare stage, one in a wheelchair and with a beard like those worn by Assyrian kings, his companion bespectacled with hair oiled back and shiny as a seal. The latter sat at a piano, while the bearded one told the audience that they were about to hear a 'farrago'. This inaugural outing of *At the Drop of a Hat*, a revue of comic banter and whimsical songs, marked the arrival of Michael Flanders and Donald Swann. The show, which didn't long dally in Notting Hill, transformed Flanders and Swann into stars and ensured that mud would henceforth become unavoidably associated with cooling the blood.

The show's opening number was entitled 'A Transport of Delight', a ditty about buses, London Transport buses, written by

the duo's librettist, Flanders. On a recording of the revue, made
by the future Beatles knob-twiddler George Martin and released
as an LP in 1960, Flanders prefaces his song with a pre-war
London bus company joke: 'Well, buses . . . we had one outside
here, about twenty minutes ago with private on it, looking very
lost. I can remember when it was a General.' Boom. Boom. I
guess you had to be there; on the album there's an effusive chortle, followed by a clatter of audience applause. Flanders, who
contracted polio in 1943 after his destroyer was torpedoed, would
have found it extremely difficult – no, impossible – to get on *any*
London Transport bus, including the prototype Routemasters.
(After the war, his disability had barred him from resuming his
place at Christ Church College, Oxford.) So in retrospect the
joke has an air of pathos about it, as well as an antiquity only
added to by a minor anachronism in the lyrics – all the diesel
buses in the song have six wheels, a common feature on pre-war
models.[34]

Still, the lyrics provide a barometer of contemporary attitudes
toward London buses and their drivers and conductors, just as
their song *The Reluctant Cannibal* may do about race.[35] The song
portrays bus crews (the duo adopting the roles of driver and clippie) as venal wage-grabbing road hogs who contrive, wherever
possible, to keep other vehicles from overtaking them and passengers from boarding their buses:

---

34   Trolleybuses did have six wheels but London Transport's LT 6-wheelers retired
     in 1950.
35   'I suppose you realize, son,' quips Flanders, who in this song is a chieftain
     whose offspring declines to eat humans, 'that if this gets around we may never
     get self-government.'

Along the Queen's great highway
I drive my merry load
At twenty miles per hour
In the middle of the road;
We like to drive in convoys
We're most gregarious;

And it continues:

I stops when I'm requested
Athough it spoils the ride,
So he can shout: 'Get aht of it!
We're full right up inside!'

We don't ask much for wages,
We only want fair shares,
So cut down all the stages,
And stick up all the fares.
If tickets cost a pound apiece
Why should you make a fuss?

Flanders and Swann's comic reign was relatively brief. The double act parted company in 1967, when their line in animal gags and urbane and very English observation had come to be seen as rather quaint in the new harder age of satire. But the sentiments of 'A Transport of Delight' were prescient in many respects. Wages, strikes, fares, levels of service and congestion would come to dominate debate about buses in the capital, with the ultimate consequence that the Routemaster would become London's last proper bus. Not that anyone could have guessed that then, when, like Flanders and Swann, the prototype Routemaster was just edging into the footlights.

At the Drop of a Hat ran for two years in the West End before transferring to New York, but its success stood out against otherwise grim times for theatres in London. The Kingsway in Great Queen Street, the St James's Theatre in Jermyn Street, the Embassy in Swiss Cottage, the Stoll on Kingsway and the Tivoli Cinema in the Strand all vanished in 1956 and 1957. A few had stood empty for several years, but their destruction and replacement by office blocks was a striking indication that ways of living were changing. London was, perhaps, never more Pooteresque than in the mid-1950s. 'After my work in the City,' the Grossmiths' Mr Pooter says, 'I like to be at home. What's the good of a home, if you are never in it?'

Millions of post-war Londoners were of the same mind. A trip out to catch a show, a film or a pint in the Dog and Duck – these excursions were fast being replaced by an evening in front of the telly with a can or two of beer; 'an essential part of good living' as beer adverts of the day claimed, in earnest it would seem. (This transition from austerity to increasing affluence was caught perfectly in Richard Hamilton's 1956 pop collage, 'Just What Is It That Makes Today's Homes So Different, So Appealing?') Cinemas were especially hard hit (nationally, admissions plummeted from 1635 million in 1946 to 501 million in 1960).[36] But the effects of the new domesticity didn't bypass London

36   When the Columbia Theatre, the first new commercial cinema to be built after

Transport either. It calculated that by 1955, two years after the BBC's live broadcast of Queen Elizabeth II's coronation, 42 per cent of all households in the London Transport area had television sets. Such households, London Transport further calculated, spent 'about 5d per week less on public transport than other comparable households'.

That those families wealthy enough to buy a television might have been able to afford a car as well probably contributed to their less frequent use of bus or tube. The number of cars registered in London during the same period had nearly doubled, from 480,300 to 802,600. The situation for London Transport, whichever way you cut it, was bleak.

Like much of the nation, London Transport had long viewed the growth in car ownership as 'a natural consequence of a rising standard of living'. Though stalled by Suez (the crisis had caused petrol rationing and the suspension of driving tests), car ownership continued to rise in 1956, while the number of bus passengers continued to fall. London Transport's annual report for 1956 noted that 'in those households where the net income of the head of the house was over £20 per week only a quarter had no car or motorcycle', and that 'some 40 per cent of all cars licensed in greater London were in households in the under £10 per week category.' A review for London Transport by J Spencer Willis that year concluded that 'sweeping changes . . . have come upon us with an unprecedented swiftness . . . an enormous

---

the war, opened on Shaftesbury Avenue in 1958, it had seats for a mere 750 patrons. The State in Kilburn, which opened in 1937, seated 4004.

increase in privately owned motor vehicles, and, particularly of scooters and "mopeds", which are cheap to buy, has made more people self-sufficient in the matter of transport.'

In response to the growing number of vehicles on the roads – many of them in dubious states of repair – the government had passed its Road Traffic Act (1956), which introduced MOT tests and imposed greater restrictions on motorists; under its aegis the first parking meters would eventually be installed in Mayfair and along Oxford Street. Suez had drastically reduced congestion in London – traffic in the capital that December was reportedly down by two-thirds – and forced commuters back on to the buses. While the crisis lasted, the buses had plenty of passengers and ran, as near as damn it, on time. Once it was over they didn't.

With six-day working weeks now the exception rather than the rule, and with a greater emphasis on leisure, London Transport

felt the decline in passenger numbers most keenly at the week-ends. As it put the last of the Routemaster prototypes on the streets, it was forced to concede that there had been 'a social change in weekend pleasure pursuits; the Londoner is less inclined to go out and about unless he can do it in his own trans-port'. The cars that rolled into Earl's Court for the 39th International Motor Exhibition in 1956 were called variously 'Tourers', 'Saloons', 'Travellers' and 'Countrymen'. These were the cars for weekend voyagers; that Austin 800 cc engine and 'excel-lent luggage space' just peachy for those Sunday afternoon jaunts out of town with a full pipe clamped in your teeth, the wife at your side, a tartan blanket and a wicker hamper full of Spam in the boot, and two apple-cheeked kiddies on the backseat – con-tent, as the English countryside slipped past, to while away the hours tormenting Brambles, the family spaniel, with their pencils. I could go on but you get the gist. (Why, in 1958, with the Preston bypass, they got a motorway to picnic beside too.)

The truth is that by 1956 London was increasingly suburban, in both its tastes and where its people lived. Slum clearances and New Town and rehousing schemes at Crawley, Stevenage, Watford, Luton, Aylesbury and Hemel Hempstead were either coming to fruition or entering new phases of development. London was hardly a ghost town as a result. About 200,000 new jobs were created in central London during this period. But 150,000 of them were office jobs. London's post-war redevelop-ment plans discouraged new industrial building in the centre, the planners associating the mixture of housing and industry with images of shoeless children playing with lumps of coal among

slums. The net result was that by 1958 around 40,000 new man-
ufacturing jobs were lodged in purpose-built industrial estates in
the New Towns. What might, if you'll forgive the jargon, be called
London Transport's labour pool and its client base were both
being squeezed. With nearly full employment, the shift work and
relatively low rates of pay made a job on London's buses increasingly unattractive, no matter how attractive its new Routemaster
buses might be.

BUSMEN WANTED

In 1947, just as the design team were dusting down their drawing boards, London Transport was reaching its manning peak. By the end of that year it employed close to 100,000 people, including some 11,220 bus conductors, 8283 drivers and 803 inspectors. (Passenger numbers were at their zenith the next year.) Until the mid-1950s, there were 150 'confetti' girls at Chiswick whose job was to prepare ticket boxes for the conductors, each girl counting out the change and clippings from the returned boxes and refilling them with a fresh batch of tickets. Another 100 or so girls performed the same task for the trams and trolleybuses at London Transport's own print works on Effra Road in Brixton.

Well into the 1960s, London Transport's catering staff continued to serve over 120,000 meals daily; they had their own butchery at Griffith House in Marylebone until 1955. In the main

canteen at Chiswick, 1200 people could eat at a single sitting. 'Everything,' as a recruiting leaflet observed in 1954, 'is sold at moderate prices, just high enough to cover the cost. No profit is expected.' London Transport had its own range of subsidized staff goods under the Griffin brand name.

There was a staff hospital and two convalescent homes. Social clubs were affiliated to each garage, and the mess rooms of most of its 160 outlying canteens had dartboards and billiard tables to help the crews unwind. By 1956, London Transport owned 12 sports fields, the twelfth laid out at the Aldenham overhaul works when it opened that October.

London Transport did not neglect the minds of its employees either. There was a library at 55 Broadway presided over by two ladies who were, it is reported, 'untiring in their efforts to obtain for any applicant whatever book they wish to read on any subject'. Most garages had a designated book monitor. There was scarcely any reason to go anywhere else for rest and recreation. As one former driver said to me, 'For a time my whole life was geared around London Transport. My friends were there. My social life was there. I played sport – football and cricket, darts for the garage. And I met my wife there as well.'

A glimpse of this vanished world can be seen in the Small Items room at the London Transport Museum's Acton Depot. The Small Items room gives the distinct impression that London Transport was once a minor, and possibly totalitarian, state; some obscure Soviet republic, the People's Republic of Lodekka, whose well-ordered way of life collapsed shortly after the fall of the Berlin Wall. On display in rows and rows of glass cabinets are uniforms (spruce jackets in navy, black and grey, and shiny peaked

caps), silvery ticket machines, sporting trophies and faded photographs of sports teams and packs of Griffin tea, Griffin loo rolls
and wrappers from Griffin sausages. At Acton, a former London
Transport driver visiting from California where he'd lived for the
past 30 years[37] assured me that he ate little else other than
London Transport sausages when he was a a young carefree bachelor in Finsbury Park. 'I'd eat them at my canteen on Plimsoll
Road and then buy them to take home and fry up for my tea.' I
surmised he was a man whose stomach had always lain rather
close to his heart when he added, 'They really looked after you.
If you were out driving on the Greenline and weren't going to get
to one of the mobile canteens, they gave you a packed lunch.'

Bert Waters, who joined London Transport as a conductor shortly
after the war, recalled, 'If you worked for London Transport back
then you were respected. It was a good job. There was fair bit of
pride in wearing the uniform. Out of hours even.' Those hours
were, however, 'bloody rotten. The spread-overs were the worst. You
started at six, came off at ten and had to go back on at four in the
afternoon. Terrible.'

For conductors, the fare system could be complex. Every two
or three stops on some routes represented a change in fare rate,
and every fare change required the conductor to adjust the ticket
machine manually while also keeping a watchful eye on passengers boarding and leaving, and communicating with the driver via
the bell. At rush hour, hell.

*

37   His accent and his middle, replete with fanny-pack, were broad enough for me
      to mistake him for your stereotypical American tourist.

From 1948 onwards, London Transport found it a struggle to
attract staff. Whatever benefits it offered – Griffin sausages, smart
uniforms, subsidized canteens – didn't offset the hours, conditions
and relatively poor pay. As the post-war economy recovered,
competition for labour intensified. In 1949, London Transport's
recruiting department, unable to obtain enough employees
locally, started to cast its net wider and regularly abandoned the
confines of its offices in Griffith House, Marylebone, to tour the
provinces. The recruiting department visited Liverpool and areas
of Lancashire and Scotland where there were pockets of unemployment. Having exhausted these, it looked to Northern and
Southern Ireland, which were far more fertile ground – recruiting from Ireland persisted throughout the 1950s and 1960s.
When General Anders's Polish Second Corps was disbanded in

1950, London Transport staff were on hand at Aldershot to pick up recruits. Despite these sterling efforts and in 1954 a poster advertising campaign whose honesty and brevity owed a lot to Lord Kitchener – 'London Transport needs Men & Women Conductors' – vacancies stubbornly refused to be filled.

The Lonely Londoners, Sam Selvon's classic novel about West Indians in the capital, opens with a bus journey: 'Moses Aloetta hop on a number 46 bus at the corner of Chepstow Road and Westbourne Grove to go to Waterloo to meet a fellar who was coming from Trinidad on the boat-train.' In portraying Moses's reliance on a mode of transport that many Londoners with their mopeds and cars were beginning to avoid, Selvon was simply – although there is nothing simple about his realism – describing the everyday reality of immigrant life. Even the difficulties of the fare payer didn't escape his gaze: 'You can always tell when a test new in London – he always handing the conductor pound note or ten-shilling cause he ain't learn yet how to work out money in pounds, shilling and pence.'

Selvon's novel was published in 1956, the year London Transport began recruiting bus conductors, Underground station men and catering assistants directly from Barbados, so his decision to place the London bus at the heart of migrant life has an added poignancy. Selvon would address the subject himself in 1957 in a short story entitled *Working the Transport* about a ne'er-do-well Barbadian bus driver called Small Change: '. . . you must be reading in the papers about how London Transport send men down there in the West Indies to get fellars to work on the tube and bus, and it look as if they like Barbadians, because they didn't go to any other islands; they just get some of the boys from Little England – that is what they call Barbados down there – and bring them up to work the transport.'

London Transport's decision to recruit from Barbados had more to do with pragmatism than likes or dislikes. The Barbadian government, battling with severe unemployment, was the only Caribbean nation to approach London Transport directly about taking workers from their island, and had agreed to loan any future employees their fares.

The arrival of the SS *Empire Windrush* at Tilbury Dock on 22 June 1948 is often cited as triggering a wave of West Indian migration to Britain but the influx was modest and incremental. The British Nationality Act (1948) may have confirmed the rights of Commonwealth citizens to settle in Britain but the 1951 census records just 4200 people of West Indian birth living in London. Until 1952, when the McCarran-Walter Act closed the door to migrants, America was the preferred destination for enterprising Caribbeans. However, the decision to temporarily house those *Windrush* passengers without accommodation in the Clapham Common deep air-raid shelter, making Coldharbour Lane the nearest labour exchange, did result in Brixton (no stranger to Cypriot, Polish and Irish immigrants) becoming the first port of call for many subsequent Caribbean arrivals. In *The Lonely Londoners*, an unscrupulous Jamaican slum landlord vacuums up newcomers at Waterloo, telling them, to Bayswater resident Moses's amusement, how 'Brixton is a nice area, that it have plenty Jamaicans down there already, and they would feel at home in the district, because the Mayor on the boys' side and it ain't have plenty prejudice there.' London Transport, which opened a recruiting office in nearby Camberwell, provided work for some.

Having accepted the Barbadian government's offer, London Transport dispatched Charles Gomm, its chief recruiting officer, to Bridgetown, the island's capital, in 1956. On his first trip, Gomm, accompanied by a doctor, selected about 70 Barbadians, and trained local labour officials in London Transport's recruiting methods. Batches of workers were soon making their way to London every couple of months; more than 2000 Barbadians had been employed by the end of 1961. The scheme was extended to Malta, Jamaica and Trinidad in the mid-1960s and lasted until 1970.

In the scheme's infancy Gomm employed a welfare officer, a Barbadian, who met the new recruits as they arrived and found them suitable lodging – usually with West Indian landlords, since discrimination against blacks by white landlords was an accepted fact of life. Newcomers would then report to Griffin House, fill out the necessary forms and be treated to a suitably bumptious 'welcome aboard' lecture before they spent the next couple of days on a bus to get a feel for the city's streets. Then, after two weeks training at Chiswick, they would be assigned to a garage and sent out on the road.

Since London Transport specifically sought out unmarried men for conducting jobs, many of whom were young and away from home for the first time, the move could be traumatic. Terrible weather, cramped digs, appalling food; London and the Mother Country could cut rather a dismal prospect to begin with. Reginald Rice, a future mayor of Haringey, was 19 when he arrived on a 'grey, wet, misty day' in June and found himself sharing a boxroom in a house in Finchley with no bath or hot water.

'I can remember asking for hot water, and the landlady said the cold water's good for your complexion.'

For Gomm and London Transport, the great advantage of overseas recruitment, as Gomm said in 1992, 'was that you could put these people where you were really short of staff; I mean if I said, for example we're very short down in Southall, or Hanwell . . . we could put these people down there. And they were well received by the public'. In Reginald Rice's case this policy meant a posting to Potters' Bar in Hertfordshire, where no black community existed and where Rice would occasionally find 'Keep Potters Bar White' scrawled in the loo. The ease with which one ex-conductor felt able to tell me that he'd left one garage in the 1960s because it had 'become like bloody Calcutta' underlined some of the prejudice that black staff faced from their colleagues in those early years.

10

ALL OUT!

'To be honest,' one former conductor told me in a moment of candour, 'I always preferred the RT. It had fewer seats. On the Routemaster, you had more passengers to deal with, more hassle.' This difference in size did not escape the attention of the Transport and General Workers' Union. In the discussions that led to the Routemaster, a plan for a 70-seater bus had been dumped, precisely because London Transport feared that the unions would clamour for more money, or possibly even an additional conductor. With a closed shop, the union wielded enormous influence, holding sway over everything from the shape of the front cab (to Scott's dismay) to the number of passengers a bus might carry. Then, in May 1958, London's drivers and conductors went on strike over pay. It was a solid strike and neither side showed willingness to compromise – neither the

TGWU's leader, Frank Cousins, nor the LT chairman, Sir John Elliot.

London was only too aware of union power that summer, but at first the busmen's cause had public sympathy. That meat, butter and cheese were rotting away on barges moored on the Thames as an unofficial strike by the Smithfield transport drivers and London dockers entered its seventh week did not diminish ordinary Londoners' support for the busmen – a collection in the city on 2 June raised £88, including £5 from the porters at Covent Garden market. *Pathé News*, whose report began with the wonderful line 'Here's a picture of 8400 buses not being there', interviewed a walking cliché of a City gent (bowler hat, umbrella, a rolled newspaper wielded like Excalibur) who had a few nice words for the busmen. 'I feel,' he said, 'that they are only trying to make a better life, like we all are.' But as the strike went into June, sympathy and loyalty began to crumble. The city's public parks were turned into makeshift parking lots and commuters were encouraged to take to their cars. London was managing; a point Sir John Elliot made when he declared the strike 'a flop' and added that the heyday of the bus was gone. Congestion made it imperative, he said, to 'get people underground . . . it is our hope that some of the traffic which has gone underground will stay there.' He warned the strikers that there would be a 10 per cent cut in services and a reduction of 2500 busmen once work resumed.

In the end such radical job cuts were superfluous. By the time the strike ended, 47 days after it had begun, more than 1500 bus employees had drifted away from London Transport to find other work. The strike was a disaster for London's buses.

Shortly afterwards, London Transport calculated that 'only four-fifths of the pre-strike volume of passengers are being brought in to work in central London by the road services.' The buses' share of the traffic had fallen from 21 to 16 per cent. That November, London Transport in desperation launched a newspaper advertising campaign 'to persuade the Londoner to make better use of the bus services, to re-establish the old habit of "hopping on a bus" when time is short or weather unkind'. Appealing to the past didn't work, and in December London Transport resorted to a use-our-buses-or-you-will-lose-them campaign as services were slashed by 10 per cent. The slogan, *The Empty Seats*, was clearly intended to evoke thoughts of dear and depart loved ones and vacant armchairs by the fire, their greasy antimacassars forlornly lingering. It didn't work either. A year later, the total passenger numbers remained 8 per cent lower than before the strike. Londoners who'd made other arrangements throughout the strike – used the Underground, taken a cab, walked, cycled, bought a moped, driven their cars – weren't coming back.

When the Conservative government abolished hire-purchase restrictions in October 1958, it added to London Transport's woes; a loan to buy a car was now far easier to obtain. Since coming to office in 1951, the Conservatives had become ever more unstinting in their advocacy of the private car. Re-elected in October 1959, Harold Macmillan appointed Ernest Marples as his Minister of Transport – the same Marples who led Marples, Ridgeway and Partners, the road builders responsible for the Chiswick flyover and, soon, controversially the £1.3 million Hammersmith flyover. The first budget of the Conservatives' third term cut purchase tax. Cars were cheaper than ever before, and, with the arrival of Alec Issigonis's new Mini, more desirable to the metropolitan young.

Sir John Elliot's exhortations about 'getting people under-ground' during the strike had been aimed principally at the Ministry of Transport and the British Transport Commission. A master of obfuscation and procrastination, the ministry had delayed authorizing funds for a new Underground line from Walthamstow to Croydon – Route C, what would become the Victoria Line – which London Transport had proposed in 1952. Authority had been granted three years later but in 1959 the London Transport executive was still being asked to consider whether 'off-street parking or some other project' – a motorway, perhaps – would be 'more beneficial'. London Transport retorted

that at £55 million the cost of the Victoria Line would be 'about the same as that of an urban motorway of similar length' but believed 'that its passenger-carrying capacity would be several times greater'. It was 1962 before the Conservatives gave the green light for the line, and that only after a cost analysis survey undertaken by two academics (C D Foster and M E Beesley) estimated that in reducing congestion it would benefit motorists by 35 per cent – music, one imagines, to Marples's ears.

As the decade closed, more than 30 spick and span Routemasters were rolling off the production line each month. But with 2785 driving and conducting jobs unfilled, London Transport eyed the future and prayed.

ANY COLOUR SO LONG AS IT'S RED

A few years ago I interviewed Tom Baker, the actor judged by popular consensus to have made *the best* Doctor Who. I asked him why he thought this might be the case. 'All of my episodes,' he boomed, and Baker is a boomer, 'were in colour.' A similar case could be made for the Routemaster, a child of austerity that came to prominence in the Kodacolor age. (The film was first introduced in 1957 and the company joined in the industrial exodus and shifted its main processing plant from Harrow to new larger premises in Hemel Hempstead at the end of 1959.) London in the 1950s is invariably cast as 'grey'; the shade serves as a handy mnemonic for the entire decade. The word is the opening sentence of Shaun Levy's *Ready Steady Go: Swinging London and the Invention of Cool*. Positioned alone, aloof, on the page, it's obvious, well before reading the line that follows, what era in Britain he's about to discuss or diminish or demolish. If Londoners in the 1960s felt a touch more colourful than they did in the 1950s, this was partly because the image that the city presented of itself was invariably conveyed in colour – Technicolor, Instamatic Kodacolor, *Sunday Times* Colour Section colour, James Bond colour – and not in the black-and-white of the *Lavender Hill Mob* or *Picture Post* magazine. Those famously red, open-platform double deckers would be an integral and, with more than 7000 of them in the capital, practically unavoidable feature of that giddy *mise-en-scène*.

Culturally decades are never quite as neat as their digits imply. They bleed into one another, hang over from one to the next. Tate Britain, for instance, chose to start their show 'This was Tomorrow: Art in the 1960s' by going back to 1956 – the year of a seminal ICA exhibition, 'This is Tomorrow', and the Clean Air Act (and, it goes without saying, the Routemaster's first voyage). But *Queen* magazine in September 1959 caught the spirit of the approaching decade with remarkable acuity by dubbing it 'the age of Boom'. 'Have you woken up? Do you know you are living in a new world?' it quizzed, eyebrows arched and tongue probing far into its cheek. 'You don't use words like ersatz or economy label . . . You are richer than before. You are spending more than you have ever done. Our hope is that you enjoy it. We don't want you to miss it. Don't wait till years after to realize you have lived in a remarkable age.'

In 1960 London Transport had to cope with a 6.6 per cent reduction in passenger numbers and a shortfall in drivers and conductors of 8.5 per cent. But it confirmed its faith in the

Routemaster and stated: 'It is believed that the loss of traffic on Central Road Services would have been even greater but for the replacement of the old trolleybuses with modern RM buses.' *All that Mighty Heart*, a London Transport film in full colour released two years later, positioned these sleek 'modern RMs' at the vanguard of contemporary life. In one scene, a lush green Country Routemaster carries a modish housewife (hooped skirt, bouffant hairstyle) into Stevenage New Town to do her shopping. She's off to the *new* 'self-service' supermarket in the *new* shopping centre, a beached spaceport of concrete and glass. As she loads up with tinned goods and instant coffee, our Mrs Stepford is astonished to run into an older neighbour; a twinset and pearls, bridge club type. 'Oh,' says Mrs Posh, acknowledging the younger woman's surprised countenance. 'I often come here to do my shopping *these day*s.' (Thirty years on, her offspring would be driving out to B and Q on the ring road, leaving the barren shell of the precinct to skateboarders, cider drinkers and tumbleweeds of burger wrappers.)

These days were the days of change between 1960 and 1963, when London was in love with the new. London Bridge was put up for auction.[38] Philip Hardwick's Doric Arch at Euston station was needlessly, maliciously, destroyed. Trolleybuses were swept away – the last running from Wimbledon to Fulwell on 9 May 1962. The London County Council unleashed a series of

---

38   The bridge was bought by the oil magnate Robert McCulloch and rebuilt at Lake Havasu City in Arizona. Today, you can find a Routemaster converted into an ice-cream shop, nearby.

road improvements at Euston, Elephant and Castle and the Blackwall Tunnel, intended 'to improve traffic flow and conditions, to increase capacity and to reduce delays'. One-way systems were established on Gower Street and Tottenham Court Road, Hyde Park Corner and Park Lane, while the extension of Cromwell Road and the completion of the Chiswick flyover 'more than doubled traffic' on the Great West Road and Western Avenue. The Ministry of Transport set up a working group headed by Sir Colin Buchanan 'to study the long-term development of roads and traffic in urban areas'. Published in 1963, Buchanan's *Traffic in Towns* bolstered the prevalent orthodoxy that London should be altered to give free rein to the car. (This was something of a global trend. Across the pond, Robert Moses, New York's self-styled 'Construction Co-ordinator', was ploughing a six-lane expressway through the heart of the Bronx, eviscerating the borough.) Pedestrians, Buchanan argued, were to be accommodated on a series of 'building decks' above the roads. In the meantime, office blocks rose up at Stag Place in Victoria, Notting Hill Gate, St Giles Circus and Holborn. The 26-storey Shell Centre was opened on the South Bank and construction started on Centrepoint. Traffic wardens and a profusion of new lights, signs and road markings joined the cityscape.

This 'welter of progess' is, surprising as it may seem, vividly represented in Cliff Richard's musical *The Young Ones* (1961). Richard's dad, played by Robert Morley, is a developer of office blocks, and the film's vision of London is, as the art historian David Mellor has written, 'sited between small artisanal shops, streets and youth clubs and the new high-rise buildings, continually interrupted by red blurred buses'. As London continued to refashion itself, British filmmakers who had devoted the start of the decade to pursuing 'social realism' up north, gravitated south – boarding the train with Julie Christie in *Billy Liar* (1963), as Alexander Walker once astutely observed.[39] (The Beatles followed suit, personally and then cinematically, with *A Hard Day's Night* in 1964.) Where a shot of a canal or the sound of a brass band had served as authenticity in those films, so a red double-decker bus would soon become an obligatory hallmark of any London flick.[40]

From this book's point of view, they would, of course, be . . . *the Wrong Bus*. Film companies who wanted a London bus without fail bought (or borrowed) an old RT from London Transport, as new Routemasters were replacing them. But in solidifying the association of London with a red double-decker bus, they could

---

39 I digress but . . . *Billy Liar's* director John Schlesinger cut his teeth making *Terminus*, a British Transport Commission documentary charting a day in the life of Waterloo station. In *A Kind of Loving*, his first feature, filmed in Yorkshire, the romance between Vic (Alan Bates) and Ingrid (June Ritchie) is initiated on a bus, a Leyland Tiger, its ordinariness another facet of the film's 'realism'. But in *Billy Liar* Schlesinger employs several elements from his transport work, most noticeably the film's title sequence which presents a kind of bird's eye view of Britain to the strains of Godfrey Winn's *Housewife's Choice*. As in *Terminus*, *All that Mighty Heart* and *Ulysses*, the events in *Billy Liar* take place over a single day . . . but I digress.

40 Highlighting the gulf between myth and reality of the 1960s, the frequency of their appearance in films grew inversely proportional to their actual use; passengers haemorrhaging away as the city's pendulum swung. In 1966, London Transport in a public leaflet conceded that 'Monday to Friday traffic fell steadily until 1961, more gradually in 1962 and 1963, then more sharply again in 1964 and 1965.'

only contribute to the Routemaster's later reputation as the last
of its kind and an international icon.

The most fecund example of this is that other early 1960s Cliff
Richard vehicle, *Summer Holiday* (1962).[41] In this second outing
for *The Young Ones*, Cliff and the gang head Europe-wards for
some sun in a number 9 London bus. The bus in question,

---

41 *Pathé News* shot Cliff preparing for the film at Chiswick Works. England's
    answer to Elvis Presley watches an RT going through its paces on the infamous
    skidpan before taking to the wheel himself. Elvis, meanwhile, was gearing up
    to appear in *Viva Las Vegas*. The King starred as a racing driver yearning to win
    the Las Vegas Grand Prix.

    Director Peter Yates would go on to find critical acclaim for the sleek
    thriller *Bullitt* but vacuous as it was, *Summer Holiday* was the second biggest
    general release at the UK box office in 1963.

cheered and waved at by small children as it speeds, *zut alors*, for Paris, is an AEC Regent III RT. NOT A ROUTEMASTER, as I am sure you are aware.[42]

---

42   In the final episode of the 1980s alternative comedy series *The Young Ones*, *Summer Holiday*, a homage to the movie, Rick, Vyvyan, Mike and Neil do indeed plunge to their doom in a Routemaster. Sadly, though, this is a rare 'classic' TV moment for the Routemaster. Ask the average man or woman on the street – on the Clapham omnibus, as it were – to cite an appearance of a Routemaster in a film or television show and invariably *à la Summer Holiday* it will turn out to be the Wrong Bus.

Take *Here Come the Double Deckers!*. This television series, originally aired in 1970, is fondly remembered, along with Olde English flavour Spangles, by thirty–forty somethings with too much disposable income and a paucity of taste. The programme charted the zany japes of a Secret Seven-ish gang of irrepressible kids whose clubhouse was a mothballed London bus. The stars included a young Brinsley Forde (later of the Reggae group ASWAD) and a not so Young One Melvyn Hayes. The bus, needless to say, was not a Routemaster but an RT.

Double Deckers creator Harry Booth then went on to direct the first two of three (yes, three) feature film spin-offs from *On the Buses*, London Weekend Television's execrable Reg Varney sitcom.

The past, when it comes to England in the early 1970s, is not so much a different country but a lost continent and one for which the surviving maps fail to convey anything like a convincing representation of its buxom dolly bird-fixated topography. In 1971, Booth's *On the Buses* movie beat *Diamonds are Forever* (Sean Connery's final 'official' performance as James Bond) to become the nation's highest box office earner. The sideburned Reg played the wily bus driver Stan Butler, while Bob Grant played his lecherous clippie Jack Harper. Grant was an actor who had once worked as a bus conductor, though his distinctive haystack locks, Concorde nose and equine teeth would have made him ideal for the part of Tufty had RoSPA ever felt compelled to produce a live action version of their do-gooding squirrel's road safety adventures. A Britain where such people were sexually attractive to pneumatic young 'lookers' in micro-minis may have been a kinder place for unattractive middle-aged men to inhabit. But it wasn't a sane one. (Hammer held a nationwide competition to choose the title of the second *On the Buses* film. The winning entry? *Mutiny on the Buses*.)

Though RTs and Routemasters do sneak into the films – there's a 'hilarious' incident featuring Blakey, the Hitler-moustached Inspector, together with Chiswick's skidpan and a skidding Routemaster – the series itself was set

Summer Holiday begins pointedly in black and white; grey, if you like. In the opening title sequence a uniformed brass band,

---

outside London. Butler drives a green number 11 bus to 'Town's End' for the Luxton and District Traction Company – his route terminates at the cemetery gates. Luxton operates in the Home Counties somewhere (there are posters for Southend dotted about the depot) and in keeping with the locale has a fleet of dodgy provincial buses. Most of them, aptly for an era when *double entendre*, as opposed to today's irony, was the chief comic device, were Bristols.

Could being trounced by *On the Buses* in 1971 have perhaps encouraged the director of *Diamonds are Forever*, Guy Hamilton, to include in his next Bond feature, *Live and Let Die*, a chase sequence on a Caribbean island involving a London bus? Who can say – but from the instant Roger Moore assumed the role the Bond franchise certainly acquired a cricked neck from emulating whatever film genres and trends happened to be rattling the cash registers at the time, so it's conceivable. To watch these vintage Moore Bonds now is to be treated to a masterclass in popular 1970s cinema: *Live and Let Die* (1973) is Bond does Blaxploitation; *The Man with the Golden Gun* (1974) is a Kung Fu picture; the aquatic environs, sharks and steel-toothed villain of *The Spy Who Loved Me* (1977) salute *Jaws* and *The Poseidon Adventure*; and in *Moonraker* (1979) Bond, after some star wars, has close encounters with Dr Holly Goodhead in outer space.

Still, none of this alters the fact that the double decker that 007 and the comely psychic Solitaire (Jane Seymour at her winsome best) commandeer to elude Kananga's henchmen in *Live and Let Die*, slicing off its top deck as they race under a low bridge, is an RT. (With a top speed of 40 mph, it joins the 2CV, a Moon buggy and a 3-wheeled tuk tuk taxi in the canon of unrealistic but effective Bond getaway vehicles.)

And it's no use pointing to that episode of *Some Mother's Do 'Ave 'Em* where the hapless Frank Spencer is dragged up a high street on his roller skates by a red London double decker either. It's an RT-type too.

That triple-decker purple thing – the Knight Bus – in *Harry Potter and the Prisoner of Azkaban*? An RT.

Of course, there are stacks of street scene cameos in the likes of *Blow Up*, *The Sweeney*, *Minder*, *The Bill*, *EastEnders* etc – and an episode of *Sykes* in which Hattie Jacques and Eric Sykes are conductress and driver on a Routemaster – but it's slim pickings really.

Sorry. I have an inkling there was one in *Notting Hill*, but nothing could induce me to see that film again.

The actor Stephen Lewis in character (i.e. gurning as if his life depended on it) as Inspector 'Blakey' Blake from *On the Buses*. Blakey was a stickler for the rules. He had a Hitler moustache. Subtle, wasn't it?

stiff old duffers to a man, stand on the beach of an endearingly
dreary English seaside resort[43] and oompah-oompah their way
through the theme song till a downpour forces them to abandon
their performance and rush for cover. The lachrymose tune then
resumes with Cliff's dulcet tones and Hank Marvin's guitar at the
helm. A rheumatism-inducing montage of flooded promenades,
sodden cricket grounds and overflowing storm barrels flits by.
With the wetness of English weather established beyond argu-
ment, a rain-lashed Aldenham bus works finally fills the screen.
Inside the works Melvyn Hayes and his cohorts indulge in some
speak-the-plot lines while munching sarnies (eschewing what was
by all reports a very impressive canteen). 'Isn't the English
weather beastly?' and 'Where are we going for our holiday?' and
'I think Cliff's got something up his sleeve' . . . dialogue of that
sort, before at long last the Bachelor Boy, driving a double-decker
bus, looms into view. Suddenly, just like in *The Wizard of Oz*, the
picture bursts into vibrant colour. The fantasy that would engulf
the decade can begin. Like Dorothy with her ruby slippers, these
'fellers' and their scarlet bus are off to make new friends and
encounter colourful characters in exotic lands: Lauri Peters, Ron
Moody and Greece.

The dance number 'Seven Days to Our Holiday' that ensues
while, in what must have been a gross breach of standing union
and London Transport productivity agreements, the boys trans-
form the bus – in their own time, using works equipment?
I should coco – into a caravan, does give a keen sense, however

---

43   Tony Hancock's *The Punch and Judy Man* was made in the same year. Did
      English hoteliers and seaside-rock manufacturers picket the cinemas in 1963?

airbrushed, of Aldenham in action. Bus bodies glide through the air, winched effortlessly through this vast hangar of a building on overhead tracks, and teams of workers heigh-ho, heigh-ho their tiny hearts out as they step purposefully about the floor in overalls, carrying tools.

Aldenham employed around 2000 staff then and overhauled over 40 buses a week – every London bus was overhauled every four years. Another reason why the Routemasters lasted so well. The bodies and chassis (technically, as you'll recall, two frames on Routemasters) were separated when they arrived – and were unlikely to be reunited again once this was done. The chassis were completely dismantled and rebuilt with replacement parts fitted as required. As all the parts were standardized, to save time and money each repaired body – and body repair usually took longer – was slotted on to whatever chassis came off the line next. Completed buses were whisked, 12 at a time, by a conveyor belt to the paint shop and treated to two coats of paint, varnished, the adverts refreshed. Now they were ready to go back on the road, as good as new, or nearly.

It looks very jolly in the film. But what was it like to work there? Brian Watkinson, who was employed in the accident shop in the 1960s, told me it was 'a unique place to work' and 'very different to Chiswick because of its isolation from the rest of London Transport'. That isolation, it's clear, bred an unmistakable camaraderie at Aldenham. Aldenham maintained its own lively sports and events calendar. The dance floor in its social club was judged among the staff to be 'the best in Hertfordshire' and witnessed many a heady shindig in its prime. Working conditions in certain areas would, however, have had Melvyn and chums praying for rain. The lower saloon repair bay was the worst area, according to Watkinson. 'Most of the work was on one's knees and there was little ventilation, so it got very hot in the summer.'

Filmed in 1962, *Summer Holiday* acknowledged the arrival of cheap foreign holidays for all. Our guys 'n' girls take a piece of London along with them; those who came later would be haunting faux cockney boozers on the Costa del Sol. For the drivers and conductors, the allocation of holidays was yet another contentious issue and one, at a time when leisure was fast becoming the primary motivating force of young Britons, that made the job steadily less attractive.

Holiday firms in those dark days generally assumed that everyone worked a five-day Monday-to-Friday week. To maximize your time off, you lugged your suitcase to Blackpool, Butlins Bognor or Benidorm, on a Saturday. A week or two later, you came home, a sombrero perched on your head, a little toy donkey under your arm, and a suitcase that looked like a python digesting a camel. Simple. LT holidays, on the other hand, ran from Sunday to Saturday.[44] A crew member who wanted to start his holiday on a Saturday might have to swap a rest day with a colleague or pull a sickie, causing immense aggravation in the summer months when no one wanted to work on a Saturday anyway.

Summer Holiday, with its mix of 'ye olde London bus' and its

---

44   This practice lasted until 1965 when their six-day working weeks were also shortened to five days.

'young ones', represented everything that Britain had wanted to project since Suez – 'tradition and progress' had been the nation's official theme at the Brussels Exhibition four years earlier (and not for the first or last time). But the notion of using a London bus to promote Britain as a modern thrusting nation and as a tourist destination was really pioneered at the Festival of Britain. The Festival, intended as a world trade fair to mark the centenary of the Great Exhibition, had been scaled down to a national festival as part of Stafford Cripps's austerity regime. So that the rest of the world did not miss out, four gleaming new RT buses (three equipped with exhibition displays, and carrying leaflets in eight languages; one bus for the staff and spare parts) drove around Scandinavia and mainland Europe for three months in the summer of 1950. Back from their 'Summer Holiday', they were deployed as sightseeing buses for the festival, offering two-hour 'Around the town for half a crown' tours.[45]

The following March, three London double deckers were dispatched to the United States to support a 'Come to Britain' campaign organized by the British Travel and Holidays Association. (Transatlantic rapprochement was in the air in 1952; Churchill had visited Truman in Washington that January to renew Britain and America's 'special relationship'.) The double deckers travelled from New York to San Francisco and back and through the Eastern Provinces of Canada, and clocked up more than 12,000 miles.

You might think of these excursions as crusades against London's image of greyness; against, for example, the work of the Zurich-born photographer Robert Frank, who reached London

---

45   One of the buses was on display at the Greenwich Dome in 2000.

Swinging London: A Routemaster being loaded onto a ship
bound for Oslo at Millwall Docks in April 1966.

from Paris in 1951. Frank described the city as 'black, white and gray' and his monochrome photographs certainly exemplify that description. His pictures of City gents in their long black coats and bowler hats are silhouettes against a fug of grey; Charles Bridge statues tailored by Gieves and Hawkes. In one of his finest street scenes, a Magritte-like figure prowls through the City, with his arms and a newspaper tucked martial-style behind his back. Ahead of him, to the right, is a number 25 bus. It's paused at a stop and a woman is climbing aboard the rear platform. Until very recently, this photograph graced the Penguin edition of Evelyn Waugh's *Scoop*, a novel first published in 1938.

But if 1951 could stand in for 1938, it couldn't do the same for 1962. Ten years after Frank's visit, the Hungarian Erwin Fieger shot the same bowler-hatted gents, the same buses and the same streets, but in colour. The lethal smog has gone. The fuzziness in his polychromatic London is supplied by motion: the red of a bus's reflection bleeds all over a stationary London cab, dyeing its paintwork crimson, and in another picture puts a halo round a pipe-smoking man to make crisp the bristles of his moustache. Fieger's photographs were published with a text by the novelist Colin MacInnes as *London City of any Dreams* (1962), a book which depicts an old town absorbing the new. Featured on the front cover is a photograph of a young woman in an elegant white mac and headscarf, at the taxi rank at Victoria station. She's adjusting the scarf nonchalantly, a bag hangs loosely from her left hand, and scarlet and black surround her; a 134 bus[46] acts as the backdrop and the outline of a cab as

---

46   Sadly, an RT by the look of the windows.

the frame. With her poise and her swagger, she could be Julie Christie skipping down from Yorkshire a year or two early.[47] The picture screams: London, confidence, youth, beauty, mobility . . . in colour. A saturated fat, full English breakfast colour. A London bus has never looked redder. It can only be the 1960s. (The headscarf and heavy eye make-up are, I concede, a bit of a giveaway too.)

That same year, the pop artist Allan Jones was working on a sequence of bus canvases utilizing comic book-style graphics and thick daubs of red and flashes of yellow paint to evoke the vehicles in motion. (His *2nd Bus* could easily have provided the basis for the sleeve of The Beatles' *Yellow Submarine*.) The London bus was on the road to becoming a pop icon.

In November 1962, a major survey of contemporary British art opened at the San Francisco Museum of Modern Art. Entitled 'British Art Today' it featured works by the likes of Richard Smith, John Plumb, Brian Wall and Patrick Heron, and was one of the first exhibitions of British 'Pop Art' in America. The show was trailed by 'London Week', a cultural/trade jamboree that recast San Francisco 'as Francis Drake had always intended' as New Albion. 'Everything is pip-pip and tickety-boo in San Francisco,' was *Pathé News*'s verdict. Their bulletin included a town crier, a bobby and a mini-skirted beefeater (beefette, could it be?) accosting passersby in Union Square. And also a Routemaster, shipped over for the occasion, darting between the cable cars on the city's famous hills.

*

---

47   OK. Wrong station.

Lost in translation: a Routemaster on the streets of Toyko in the 1960s.

The Routemaster was in its boom age. More than 1000 had been built by this time[48] and new ones were appearing at a rate of about eight a week. In its infancy London Transport engineers had waged a ceaseless battle just to keep the Routemasters on the road – the bus was plagued at first by an array of bugs and faults: the front tyres, shock absorbers, radiator fans and brake shoes

---

48   When the thousandth Routemaster rolled off the production line on 16 October 1961, the man given the honour of driving it, a Mr Edwin Thomas Bonny, had worked for the firm, through its various incarnations, for 50 years, having signed up at 15 as an apprentice mechanic. The conductor for the day, Mr Edmund William Robson, had a mere 39 years' service. Both men, naturally, were presented with commemorative ashtrays.

wore poorly, the bell would (somehow) interfere with the gears, and the windscreen wipers were infuriatingly unreliable. These glitches were finally being eradicated. The Routemaster, locally and internationally, was becoming London's ace face at a time when London was *the* place to been seen. Oh so quintessentially, classically British and yet modern; it was *The Avengers* on wheels. Prior to San Francisco, the Routemaster, performing its role as a diesel-powered beefeater, had dropped in on Switzerland, Holland and France. Trips to Germany, Austria, Belgium, Norway and Japan would follow.

12

OR MAYBE NOT

London Transport engineers were tinkerers by nature, seekers of perfection. The Routemaster was never an end in itself as far as the bods at Chiswick were concerned, and in the opening years of the 1960s, in the spirit of the *Zeitgeist*, they pursued new ideas, ran flags up poles and stormed their brains. The Routemaster got longer, a fleet of coach versions was commissioned and plans for a front-entrance model were drafted. But there was one itch that wouldn't go away. How could they make the Routemaster lighter? What could they take off it which wouldn't impair the comfort of the passengers or its performance on the road?

The answer had been staring them in the face all the time. Its paint. Those scarlet tunics, it was calculated, added about 3 cwt (152.4 kg) to the bus. Why not just forget about paint? Painting the buses took time and money. Why bother if bare aluminium did the job just as well? Yuri Gagarin had returned from space. John F Kennedy had vowed to have 'a man on the moon' by the end of the decade. An 80 ft wide stainless-steel cube was being erected on the roundabout at the Elephant and Castle. London could have a bus fit for the space age. An unpainted aluminium Routemaster, christened the 'Silver Lady' by its garage staff, landed on the capital's streets in July 1961 on the route from Victoria to Edmonton.

This was a risky move; the colour of London's buses was sacrosanct. 'We expect,' a London Transport press release admitted, 'that it will cause some controversy and we shall invite the public, by a notice in the bus, to write and tell us what they think.' Historically, London buses hadn't always been red and were once a multitude of hues – in the pirate years of the 1920s London had seen a profusion of wildly coloured buses. Before the Second World War, London Transport's own red buses often had their window frames and roofs in cream.[49] With the RTs and Routemasters, that contrast shrivelled to a thin white band below the top deck and red became the dominant colour. (Green on the Greenline and Country services, of course.) Up until the Edwardian period colours rather than numbers had indicated a bus's route.

London from the Top of a Bus, an illustrated guidebook

---

49 You can still spot the occasional bus with this style of livery in Alexander Mackendrick's *The Ladykillers* (1955), a rare colour outing for Ealing Studios. The dark greys, purples and greens of the sooty roads behind St Pancras are intermittently enlivened by the flash of a red bus in the distance; its steady passage another sign, perhaps, along with the steam trains, that the indefatigable Mrs Wilberforce will triumph over Professor Marcus and his eccentric gang.

The girls go crazy for all-over bus advertising in 1969.

published in 1906,[50] includes a list of the capital's buses and
identifies them by their destinations and by the colour of their
paintwork: light green, dark green, dark blue and red. Under this
loosely chromatic scheme, vehicles of different colours stuck to

---

50 Written by A St John Adock, its unique selling point was that it had photo-
    graphs taken, as its author insisted, 'from the roof of the moving 'bus, whilst
    it was going its usual journey, and therefore represents the views as they are
    actually seen by the passenger from the bus top'. A perusal of the out-of-focus
    images it contains makes you consider if London really did present itself as a
    frenetic blur to early motorbus passengers weaned on the horse. Or was the
    camera, or the photographer Henry Irving, not up to the job? Did he cheat,
    and blur them deliberately to emulate motion?

the same routes, their liveries tingeing districts like the squares on a Monopoly board. This wasn't really a system per se and overlapping was common. In the 1890s, for instance, in a war over territory, the London General and the London Car Company pitched their blue and orange buses against one another on the same Brondesbury to Putney route. German visitors to London found this sort of thing most confusing. Or at least members of the Baedeker family did, as any clan whose guides specified the thickness of tweed required for Swiss hill-walking probably would. To make life easier for tourists, Baedeker allocated its own 'unofficial' numbers for each bus route in its London handbook. The Vanguard bus company adopted the idea, and on 23 April 1906, the 4 from Gospel Oak to Putney station became the first bus in London to sport a route number. Routes 3–1 followed retrospectively, and numbering became universal from1908 onwards, by which time the General was settling on a standard red livery for its fleet. London Bus red – Pantone 485.[51]

---

51   In 1969 London Transport was approached by Silexine Paints. The company
     wanted to organize an art contest for young students to help publicize its
     paints; the winning design, on a London theme, would be painted over a whole
     bus and used to promote tourism. (Q. As the bus ran only in London, weren't
     any visitors who saw it in the city there already?) The winner, a predictable
     mélange of biscuit tin leitmotivs (Guardsmen, the Houses of Parliament, whelk
     salesmen etc) accompanied by the rejoinder *Silexine Paints Welcome You to
     London*, was daubed on to RM1737 in the summer of 1969 and unveiled with
     a gaggle of pop-sock-clad hip chicks outside the Chelsea Drugstore. The fash-
     ion for all-over adverts spread like a virus in early 1970s, with *Yellow Pages*,
     Meccano, Hanimex Cameras and Spiller's Homepride outdoing one another
     in garish paint jobs. The last drew a public complaint from an outraged peer
     of the realm who'd missed a number 15 bus in the West End after mistaking
     it for a bread van.

In 1961, this colourful past a folk memory, Londoners hated the Silver Lady. Of the 263 letters London Transport received about the bus, 226 were, as they delicately put it, 'unfavourable'. It was repainted red.[52] An anecdote burnished to a sheen by its repeated use suggests that public outrage had little to do with its withdrawal; in foggy conditions the bus vanished from sight.[53]

---

52 A stipulation of the 1994 privatization of London buses was that 80 per cent of central area vehicles should be painted London Bus Red. Following partial deregulation in 1988, the Grey-Green company – whose Volvo buses (unsurprisingly) sported crushingly maudlin gunmetal grey and green paintwork – won the tender for route 24 from Victoria to Hampstead Heath, which passed through Parliament Square. The sight offended some Tory grandees, who found their love of free market liberalism at odds with their inbred fetish for tradition and fox-hunting red.

53 In 1977, 25 Routemasters were painted silver and wheeled out for the Jubilee celebrations.

13

ONE MAN, ONE BUS

Everyone had a chance to buy their own Routemaster bus in 1964. 'Seats, staircase, handrail, spring suspension, driver and clippie, jewelled headlights,' proclaimed the text on the yellow and powder blue box of the Corgi Toys diecast 'London Transport Routemaster bus'. Destination: London Bridge.[54] (Rivals Dinky were in on the act too.) Buses come and go but toys last a lifetime – or have done ever since the *Antiques Roadshow* was first screened. Popular as the Corgi Routemasters were, the kids of '64, fickle, foolish creatures, elected to throw more of their hard-cadged pocket money at the Citroën Ski Safari Winter Olympics, with its roof rack and detachable skis, and the Bedford

---

54   The Austin Driving School Car, which came with the junior *Highway Code*, was another addition to the Corgi range that year.

'Chipperfield's' giraffe transporter – two giraffes included. These were toys with extra bits. Extra bits bound to get lost down the back of the sofa,[55] causing tears, recriminations and gradual abandonment. In the toyshop they had looked exciting, better value.

Small children we can forgive, but London Transport acted with equal fecklessness when it took a decision in 1964 to pursue the faddish and to save cash. Since the 1958 strike, arguments about bus crews' pay and conditions had smouldered on. In 1960, London Transport had made substantial wage increases, to no real avail. Staff shortages had been further exacerbated by trolley-buses' drivers and conductors, unhappy about changing working practices, drifting away from the service. Bill Reynolds was one such trolleybus driver. 'I hated the blinking sight of them Route-masters. I was at Fulwell, left the same day they arrived in '62. Quite a few of us did. As far as I remember, couple of fellars stayed but most of us went. It was a real chalk and cheese thing, you know, you didn't mix with bus drivers and conductors. We had our union, our depots, they had theirs, we had our way of working, they had theirs. We didn't want anything to do with them.[56]

Where trolleybus and bus garages merged, as they did at Bow and Clay Hill, staff kept their distance, sitting at opposite sides of the canteen. The bus drivers' and conductors' own union representatives were unhappy, too, about the replacement of RT

---

55 Usually during *Doctor Who*.
56 'Oh, yes, I quite like them now of course,' Bill said, when I asked about the
    Routemaster. He was, at the time I spoke to him, attending the Routemaster
    50th rally in Finsbury Park.

buses with the larger Routemasters, and negotiations over greater productivity had floundered. The union felt their members should share in some of the cost benefits if London Transport intended to run fewer buses. In 1962 the Ministry of Transport established a committee headed by the economist Sir Ernest Henry Phelps Brown to review the whole issue of busmen's (and buswomen's) pay and conditions.

Published in January 1964, the Phelps Brown Report outlined a few stark truths. 'We now have full employment. The driving of buses, working shiftwork and having to work at weekends when other people are enjoying themselves is not attractive and earnings here proved insufficient to compensate for the disabilities of the nature of the employment.' The busperson's lot was not, it was stated, without its perks. 'There is an absence of monotony, the contact with people is an attraction for many, and

the freedom from direct and continuous supervision gives the driver and conductor an independence which cannot be found in factory life.'

The Routemaster was singled out for special praise. 'The Routemaster bus now being placed in service is probably the most advanced in the country, and we would claim that on no other vehicle in use has so much attention been given to the convenience of both the driver and the conductor. The driver's cab, including the seat, layout of driving controls and auxiliary switches, has been designed scientifically as a result of operational research into the work of the driver.' But here the report took a more contentious line, placing the blame for failures in the network squarely on the busworkers. 'It has not been possible so far to reach an agreement with the staff to enable the full potentiality of these vehicles of advanced design and for improvements in operating efficiency to be reached.' The previous February during negotiations over pay, 'the men' had 'preferred a lesser flat increase rather than acceptance of the principle of increased productivity'. At the committee hearings, Mr Henderson of the TGWU argued that although they had rejected the deal on offer, they had 'always been willing to join with the board in negotiations in regards to measures of efficiency . . . whether it be bigger buses, one-man buses or any other measure.'

In an industry beset by staff shortages, one-man buses were viewed as a panacea. The idea of getting rid of the conductor was difficult to resist, and perhaps understandable/forgivable in the context of an epoch where supermarkets, vending machines and off-the-peg 'boutiques' were shaking up norms of behaviour. (Automatic vending machines for tea had been installed, 'experimentally', at 55 Broadway and Enfield Garage as early as 1960.) London Transport estimated that about '20,000,000 miles per year' were being lost due to staff shortages and it was desperate to find a solution. One-man operation, or OMO (later OPO, one-person; Jill Viner, the first woman bus driver in London, wasn't employed until 1974) on single-decker buses had taken off in the provinces and it was used by London Transport on some of its Country routes.

London Transport had trialled a 'Pay as You Board' system 'retaining a conductor in the manner found on the continent' back in 1944, but it was inefficient and unpopular. Although one-man operation on double deckers was illegal at the time for safety reasons, Leyland and Daimler were pioneering a range of front-entrance, rear-engined double deckers which they asserted could easily be operated by the driver alone. Leyland was very much in the ascendancy during this period; in June 1962 it had merged with (ie gobbled up) the Associated Commercial Vehicles Group – which included AEC and Park Royal – to form the Leyland Motor Company. The result was that the Routemaster – body, engine and frames – became a product of the Leyland conglomerate. Within months of the Phelps Brown report, Leyland's super salesman Donald Stokes would pull off an audacious deal, selling £9 million worth of Olympian buses to Cuba – flouting the US government's trade embargo.[57]

The report stated that 'several new' types of vehicle were 'under consideration' – an indication that LT was weighing up off-the-shelf manufacturers' models. But a press briefing on

---

57   'Raymond Baxter, an ex-British Motor Corporation man, and later *Tomorrow's*

23 March 1958 made it plain that London Transport had been under pressure to justify the expense of commissioning vehicles specifically for London for some time. In the light of what would follow, this briefing is worth quoting from.

'It had often been asked (Mr Durrant said) why London Transport felt it necessary to incur expenditure on the design and development of a special bus of its own, and why it did not go to the bus industry and let it spend the money on the project. This, it had been suggested, would save the cost to London Transport. Mr Durrant explained that the size of London's transport fleet was such that the numbers of vehicles involved were sufficient to enable a specially designed bus to be produced efficiently and economically. Also, the conditions of operation in London were quite peculiar to the capital, and important economies could be achieved by using a vehicle designed to meet these conditions closely.'

Engineers at Chiswick, conscious of the trend toward forward entrances had created a front-entrance Routemaster, RMF1254, and unveiled it at the Earl's Court Motor Show in 1962. Treated to a cool reception by the union, it was judged unsuitable for central use but 50 were ordered by the Northern General Transport of Gateshead – who became the only bus company outside

---

World presenter, observed in an interview in 2002 that the fact that Stokes 'was selling them at knockdown prices, and there was no profit at all, and the buses weren't any bloody good either, was neither here nor there. The name of Stokes was legion.'

London to operate Routemasters. (At £9000 a pop, Routemasters were around a grand more than your average provincial bus in the 1960s.) Even with a front door, the design of the Routemaster's cab precluded the driver from collecting fares. To deal with boarding passengers, a complex swivel chair would have been needed, which could, perhaps, have lent a raffish Bond villain charm to the proceedings (cue squeak of leather . . . 'Good evening, Mrs Bass, I've been expecting you. The White Horse, East Ham, I presume? That will be . . . one m-m-m-million pounds . . .' cue maniacal laughter) but would have been utterly impractical.

Having sifted through the evidence, London Transport's board decided that 'there may well be considerable scope for the use of one-man operation in the suburban fringe of the central area.' There was obviously some trepidation about preparing this announcement. The original press statement, a copy of which is on file in the London Transport Museum's library, reads: 'there is considerable scope'; the typed 'is' has been vigorously scribbled out and the more qualified 'may well be' added in pencil over the top.

In conclusion, the board 'considered a double-deck vehicle of front-entrance type, so designed that the upper deck could be closed during off-peak periods, when it would be operated as a one-man vehicle, was the most hopeful way of matching the crew and vehicle to the changing pattern of traffic through the day.' These lines were, in effect, a death sentence for the Routemaster.

ALFIE: WHAT IT WAS ALL ABOUT

On 23 February 1965, London Transport issued the first of what quickly became a flurry of public statements about London's buses. 'For some time now,' it began, 'the outlook for London bus passengers has seemed bleak. There have been too few buses when most people have wanted to use them; buses have been waiting crews to man them.' To resolve this problem, London Transport boasted that a 'more efficient and economical deployment of that scarce commodity – manpower' had been established. Routemasters were still, for the moment, being built – 65 front-entrance models were manufactured for British European Airways (BEA), who used them to shuttle air passengers back and forth between Cromwell Road and Heathrow Airport – but trials of new off-the-shelf single-decker AEC Merlins and double-decker

Daimler Fleetline and Leyland Atlantean buses for one-man operation were started.

In April 1966, *Time* declared London the 'Swinging City'. On the
magazine's cover a cartoon tableau of the groovy metropolis in
action, and there, tucked beneath Big Ben, was a red double-
decker bus with the words 'Join the Tea Set' emblazoned on its
side.[58] Boston was water under the bridge, and all that. One of the
hordes of Americans who beat a path to the capital in the aftermath of the *Time* piece was the pop-singer daughter of Ole Blue
Eyes, Nancy Sinatra. 'I was one of the first people to wear the
Carnaby Street mini-skirt in Hollywood,' she later claimed.
Sinatra recorded the theme song for the Bond movie *You Only
Live Twice* and an album song, *Nancy in London*, on a fleeting trip
to the city in 1966. *London* kicks off with that well-known, get
out your spoons, chim chiminy sing-along 'On Broadway'. (You
can take the girl out of America . . . yada yada yada.) However,
the record's sleeve, like its title, emphasized the locale of the
recordings rather than the nature of their content. Sinatra, panda-
eyed and wearing go-go boots (what else would she be wearing?)
and a sort of yachting cap then *de jour*, is pictured sitting on the

---

58   A feature of London buses that has remained constant is advertising. In its
     opening year of trading the General coined £1223 from adverts on its vehicles.
     With Seiffert's Centrepoint rising above Tottenham Court Road and the Post
     Office Tower installed on Cleveland Street, at 620 ft then London's tallest
     building, advertisers, surmising that people would be living and working in
     high-rise blocks, thought rooftop adverts were the way forward. By early 1967,
     49 Routemasters, their roofs emblazoned with Gordon's gin ads, were whor-
     ing it around the capital.

bonnet of a Routemaster bus. This is the Routemaster as the embodiment of the swinging city – free and easy, catch me if you can, hop on and hop off, Cathy McGowan poppets clinging on to rear-platform poles.

Sadly, rather like past-its-prime Carnaby Street, buses were for losers and tourists. What most Londoners still wanted was a scooter or a fab motor. It's noticeable on *Time*'s cover that the bus passengers gawp down from the upper deck, goldfish in a bus-y bowl, at the jostling scene of fashionable and famous types, Minis, Rollers and E-type Jags below. Over the top of the bus, the name ALFIE is spelt out in lights. Lewis Gilbert's film, starring Michael Caine as the eponymous cockney Casanova ('Michael Caine IS Alfie', as the posters put it), had opened that March. As the lecherous, undomesticated barrow boy on the make, a ready stream of 'crumpet' at his tassel-loafered feet, Alfie Elkins came close to becoming a role model for bar-room misogynists across the land. The cautionary morality of the tale was perhaps lost on many, or was just much less interesting than the hedonistic male fantasy, first screening round. (Caine's performance certainly imbued a shit with an underlying vulnerability that on the basis of his actions and statements the character in the film doesn't really deserve.)

The film exposes the myth of Swinging London as much as it celebrates it, however. Grim details persistently seep through the cracks. Rented rooms are grotty, streets shabby, skins pasty, schmutter less than sharp; oily backstreet abortionists and TB clinics facts of daily life. Tellingly, it's Alfie's victims who take the bus. (Alfie is a driver, a chauffeur.) Lily, the married woman portrayed by Vivien Merchant, is advised by Alfie after her abortion

Yeah, baby, yeah.

that 'there's a bus to Waterloo or a Greenline all the way' to get her home. For the red-headed domestic goddess Annie (Jane Asher), the red double decker is a fortuitous means of escape. Her home-cooked steak and kidney pie smashed against a wall by an ungrateful Elkins, she flees the joint, hops on a departing rear platform and is away before he can reach her and pull her back. Gilda (Julia Foster) bears him a son but settles down with Humphrey, the gentle, adoring bus conductor on her regular number 19 bus[59] who is played with aplomb by Graham Stark. The spirit of the age, alas, was against chaps like Humphrey. As London Transport with its unfilled vacancies and half-empty

---

59   Nope, RT family, I'm afraid. Although Asher's bus . . . postcards please . . .

buses could have told you – there were far more self-seeking Alfies about.[60]

This was an epoch when newness was valued almost for its own sake. It practically excused the absence of all other qualities. Why else were people drinking instant Nescafé? Harold Wilson and the Labour party had come into government in 1964, promising a Britain 'forged in the white heat' of the technological revolution. London Transport was buoyed along by the currents of those high times. With the World Cup primed for kick off, Alf Ramsey's boys' bus-red shirts pressed and ready for action, London Transport released a document entitled 'Reshaping London's Bus Services'. It outlined its commitment to one-man bus operation. 'The London Transport Board believes that this method, which is already in operation in parts of their fleet, must be applied throughout the whole of the bus system as quickly as possible.'

What is it Friar Laurence says to Romeo? 'Too swift arrives as tardy as too slow.' An organization that had once devoted nine languorous years to fine-tuning the Routemaster – meticulously, painstakingly, box-tickingly – now skipped off and bought 150 AEC Merlin single deckers with the insouciance of a King's Road dandy picking up a pair of Chelsea boots. 'The wrong people,' an old Chiswick hand said to me, 'had got in charge by then.' At 8 tons 4 cwt unladen, the Merlins were significantly heavier than the Routemaster. They had standing room for 48, but they seated

---

60 The flower children who followed were not much better. In The Who's 'Magic Bus', written by Pete Townshend in 1966 and released in 1968, the lyrics are all about buying the bus from the driver rather than paying the fare.

just 25 passengers, and due to their length, 36 ft, the engineers were forced to extend the pits to service them. London Transport Authority employed them on a reasonably successful limited-stop 'Red Arrow' express service, then ordered another 500 for one-man operation without bothering to conduct wider trials. The magic wore off fast. Within ten years the entire fleet was on the scrapheap, their departure so rapid that London Transport was forced to store more than 300 of them at a disused aerodrome in Bedfordshire.

Forces in Westminster were also conspiring against the Routemaster. Barbara Castle, a non-driver, had become Transport Secretary in 1965. (Offering her the job, Wilson is alleged to have remarked, drawing on a petrol ad of the day: 'I must have a tiger in my transport policy, and you are the only tiger we've got.') Castle stayed at Transport after Labour's re-election in February 1966. On the campaign trail, she'd promised to democratize car ownership and spend more money on roads. 'If the private car has brought the boon of mobility to millions of people, which it clearly has, then that boon should be available to everyone,' she maintained, brushing aside Tony Benn's more socialist proposals for a national car-leasing scheme.

Chivvied by Richard Crossman to adopt the same kind of strategic policy to transport as he had brought to housing, Castle drafted what would be the longest piece of non-financial legisla-tion since the war. Comprising five white papers and 169 clauses, her Transport Bill, published on 6 December 1967, renationalized the bus industry – creating a National Bus Company – legalized one-man operation on double-decker buses, and introduced a system of bus grants. The grants, a 25 per cent government subsidy (subsequently increased to 50 per cent) was to operators who bought standard rear-engined manufacturers' vehicles, and effectively legislated against bespoke rear-platform buses by rendering them prohibitively expensive.[61]

Another strand in Castle's transport policy saw responsibility for London Transport pass from Whitehall to the Greater London Council, the legislative body which had replaced the London County Council in 1965. Pushed through Parliament by Macmillan and the Conservatives, the GLC was viewed, on its creation – contrary to its future reputation as Red Ken's den – as a cynical exercise in Tory gerrymandering because it extended London's city government electorate into the traditionally Conservative-voting suburbs. Desmond Plummer, Conservative head of the GLC, extracted a substantial bargain from Castle. Under the terms of the transfer, London Transport's £270 million debt would be written off by the government.[62] A series of government and GLC grants would help London Transport carry out much needed improvements, including the extension of the Piccadilly line to Heathrow. But the arrangement had a devastating effect on London's buses. The Greenline and Country bus services – which ran beyond even the GLC's dominions – were handed over to a new subsidiary of the National Bus Company, London Country Bus Services Ltd.[63] London Transport's civilizing

---

61   Castle did do some sterling work as Transport Secretary, introducing the breathalyser, preserving Britain's canals and stemming some of Beeching's rail cuts.

62   Finalized in the Transport Act (London) 1969.

63   The transfer took place on 1 January 1970. In accordance with national policy, London Country set about replacing its remaining two-person Routemasters

influence on the outer suburbs and its formerly hefty bus-buying powers were severely curtailed. It would be tougher for London Transport to argue, as Durrant had done in 1958, 'that the size of London's transport fleet is such that the numbers of vehicles involved are sufficient to enable a specially designed bus to be produced efficiently and economically'.

---

and RTs with one-man buses. In 1970, 46 per cent of its services were one-man operation, by 1975 that figure had reached 80 per cent, and was 100 per cent by the end of the decade. On the up side, London Transport reacquired many of its Routemasters and put them back into service in town, as newer and less successful buses were scrapped.

15

MAY DAY

May 1968 is remembered for its political radicalism. Across the Channel students rioted, manifestos were drawn up, petrol bombs hurled, 2CVs overturned, fists clenched, beards stroked and berets worn at revolutionary angles. There had been violent protests against the Vietnam War outside the American embassy in Grovesnor Square that March. Then in May, Swinging London held its first Festival of London Stores.[64]

The economic climate was deteriorating. Wilson had been forced to devalue the pound the previous November. The economy

---

64 When Marks and Spencer opened a branch in Paris in 1976, a Routemaster bus was ferried over for the event, and at some point in the early 1970s one Routemaster was sold to Mary Quant and transformed into a mobile boutique. It was last heard of in Finland.

was dire enough for Labour to launch its 'I'm Backing Britain' campaign to goad consumers to spend those pounds in their pockets on British goods and services. (The initiative was backed by a single by Bruce Forsyth; 'Yes I'm backing Britain', Brucey crooned, 'We're all backing Britain/The feeling is growing/So let's keep it going/The good times are blowing our way'. How could it possibly fail?)

The Festival of London Stores was conceived in much the same vein of economic desperation and received star billing in the April issue of *London Transport Magazine*. 'Each store,' it reported, 'has elected a representative for a Miss London Stores contest.' *Vive la Révolution*. Bikini-clad beauties weren't, it should be stated, the magazine's primary interest. Leading a parade through the capital for the festival on the 19 May were 'Old Bill', London General's first standard B-type bus, and the last ever Routemaster, RML2760, which had slunk off the production line at Park Royal in March. That was it. No more Routemasters. For the duration of the festival Selfridges on Oxford Street draped a banner over the entrance to its store celebrating, commemorating really, the London double decker. London Transport, like Oxford Street's shoppers, would be buying off-the-peg numbers from now on. They might not fit, the seams would come undone, they wouldn't last as long, you'd have to go off and buy another one – but that was progress for you.

With one-man operation on double deckers now legal, London Transport wanted to invest, if we want to be polite, in a fleet of new double-decker buses to replace the Routemasters and remaining RTs. Encouraging the charge to the tills was Ralph Bennett. As the general manager of transport in Manchester,

Bennett had organized the purchase of a fleet of Leyland
Atlantean and Daimler Fleetline double-decker buses. Fitted out
to his specifications, they had been promoted in the city under
the name the 'Mancunian' – nicknamed 'Bennett's Boxes'.
Bennett, who joined London Transport's board in 1968, firmly
believed that what he had devised for Manchester would be perfect for London. London Transport, which had been running trials
with prototypes of both bus models, preferred the Fleetline. And
so a version of the Daimler Fleetline (DMS) was promptly inked
in as 'London's Bus of the Future' (well, you can't let a good
slogan go to waste, can you?). A total of 1967 were ordered and
London Transport stated that by 1978 all the Routemasters – and
conductors – would be phased out. Publicized, at Bennett's suggestion, as the 'Londoner' this charmless 9 ton 15 cwt monster[65]
with its power-operated front doors and coin-in-the-slot turnstiles
first appeared in 1970, entering service in quantity in 1971. They
were proof, if proof were needed, that something had gone horribly, horribly wrong. 'The dream,' as John Lennon informed
Rolling Stone magazine that spring, 'is over.' Decimal currency had
arrived, 'Chirpy, Chirpy, Cheep, Cheep' was riding high in the
charts and now this: a London double decker which had about as
much charm and finesse as a tin of Watney's Party Seven. It was
hard to get into. You had to queue up and pay the driver[66] or jiggle
about with your 'new' coins to make them fit the slot – 'Think of
it,' proposed a London Transport advertising campaign, 'as a

---

65   The longer RML Routemasters only weighed 7 tons 15 cwt.
66   Several were crew manned and some drivers found the power steering and the
      chance to chat to the conductor and passengers a pleasant change.

phone box.'[67] And once you got inside, the experience was scarcely edifying – no Sung-yellow ceilings here.

Londoners did not fall in love with the Londoner. One driver said he detested them so intensely he swapped garages to avoid them. And the Londoner didn't, in the end, love London either. When the final RT bus – after 40 years' service – retired on 7 April 1979, the first Londoner buses were already leaving the city.

There would be others. They would be much the same. We wouldn't love them. We'd scarcely remember their names; as with a knee-trembler after one too many Cinzano Biancos we'd be left feeling ever so slightly used, tarnished by the ride somehow. We'd catch a Routemaster to be reminded of what a great double act the driver and conductor had always been: street theatre on street furniture; the Flanders and Swann, the Pete and Dud, the Lennon and McCartney of the road. In comparison, one-person buses would represent the '10', the 'Mull of Kintyre' or the 'Frog Chorus' of a less distinguished solo career. They'd seem, you know, all right at the time and we'd claim to enjoy them, sometimes. Deep inside though we knew we were lying. We'd sit down in a Routemaster, hear the bell, hand our money over to a human being – if we were lucky, one with a harmonica – and instantly we'd just know this was so much better.

It would be the same when we heard the clunk of McCartney's Rickenbecker bass on 'Rain' or caught a second or two of Pete and Dud's one-legged Tarzan sketch; we'd want them

---

67 The phone box used in the ad, coincidentally, was designed by one Douglas Scott.

all back together again, coming up with another *Revolver*. Another *Not Only But Also*. Another Routemaster. But it was too late. Things had changed. Lawyers and accountants had swooped in. So we did what we could. We loved what we had, we got carried away. And who could blame us for that? There were reissues to enjoy; it felt as if they might and should go on for ever.

16

THE BUSES WE NEVER HAD

Things could have been very different, of course. In one of his last acts before he retired in 1965, Durrant orchestrated the building of a prototype front-entrance, rear-engined Routemaster to compete with these new kids on the block. This bus was expected to be on display at AEC's stall at the Commercial Motor Show in September 1966. Visitors to the show scanned their programmes and searched in vain. It was nowhere to be seen. Like David Hemmings in *Blow Up* had they, possibly, imagined it all? The bus was eventually wheeled out for the press in December, a time of year when even the trade papers and bus fanatics, having gorged themselves on new models for months, are about as close to weary of buses as they can get. You could be forgiven for thinking someone wanted to bury FRM1, aka the Fruitmaster. Perhaps they did.

Equipped with around 60 per cent of its predecessor's components, FRM1 remains the great *what if* of London bus lore. The Fruitmaster was the last bus specifically built for London. Utilizing all London Transport's and AEC's engineering know-how, FRM1 didn't have a rear platform and had a slightly startled, rodent fascia, beady little front headlights, and a logo for a 'nose' (not unlike the original RM1). But given half the chance we could have learned to love it . . . probably. For a rear-engined, front-entrance bus, it looked a lot like the Routemaster. It had those supple curves. That bodywork. At the rear, the window was carefully recessed to disguise the engine compartment and there was a fibreglass 'bonnet' to create a tidy flat finish to its back end. At the front were a pair of doors which swished into the middle to assist two-stream boarding. It wasn't as fun as hopping on and off at the back, but at least the bus wasn't hideously ugly. (And at 8 tons 10 cwt it was a ton lighter than the Londoner.)

It entered public service on 26 June 1967, running on route 76, and although its engine suffered a fire, passengers liked it – drivers at Tottenham garage, where it was based, were so enamoured of it that they drew lots to determine who got the chance to take it out.

But FRM1 was doomed. Park Royal and AEC were now part of Leyland and Leyland was perfectly happy with its own new rear-engined, front-entrance Atlantean bus. Sir Donald Stokes, the super salesman, didn't want AEC wasting its energies on a front-entrance Routemaster. London Transport was fixated on single deckers, and the Fruitmaster, with Durrant gone, withered on the vine. It never got beyond a single prototype. Banished to the suburbs for much of its working life, FRM1 spent its dotage as a London tour bus. If FRM had gone into production, would the Routemasters have survived in London as long? We can never know.

In 1975, after nearly a decade of inflicting substandard off-the-shelf buses on the capital, London Transport announced a four-year plan to develop a new double-decker bus. Engineers hatched bold ideas; setsquares, pencils and spanners twitched in feverish activity, skies turned blue from all the unfettered thinking. Here at last was a chance to come up with a bus fit for London in the 1980s.

They dubbed it XRM. It would have eight wheels and a low floor for full disabled access. They'd put the engine under a central staircase, so the buses could have one or two doors if you wanted them and still keep . . . a rear platform. And a conductor, if you liked. It was a bus for the future, that hadn't forgotten the past.

Did we get it? Of course not. By the time Londoners were brushing asymmetric fringes out of their eyes to the strains of 'Don't You Want Me Baby', the project was history. And so were Park Royal and AEC; British Leyland rationalized the Southall plant out of existence in 1979 and Park Royal closed in 1981.

PART 2

17

SOMETHING TO TELL THE KIDS

Tyburn Way, by Marble Arch, is one of those spots in central London, a little like that useless pond under Centrepoint, that's easy to see and tricky to reach. Subsumed in the Marble Arch traffic island complex, a scrubby nexus of monuments, roads, concrete barriers and ornamental flowerbeds, it's hemmed in on all sides and is only really accessible via an underpass that sprouts off from the tube. Once the site of mass hangings and Tyburn's Triple Tree gallows, its most regular visitors now are the bus crews who pull up beside the wall there for short breaks. Here the drivers and conductors can grab a quick fag and stretch their legs on the grass, undisturbed by would-be passengers and direction-seeking tourists.

Black Friday, 3 September 2004 was different. It was the last day for the Routemasters on routes 390, 9 and 73, and the crews had an audience. A large throng of enthusiasts had gathered on the verge and were observing their every move, taking photographs and notes as the Routemasters approached, with the rapt gaze of fashionistas surveying the latest catwalk collection.

Odish Ciceki, a conductor on the 390, looked on in bemusement at the crowd as he perched on the wall and rolled a cigarette. A neat, compact man with a trim, grey moustache, sunglasses and a Nehru-style hat, Odish could have passed for an international diplomat if it hadn't been for the roll-up. He'd been conducting for the past seven years and was taking early retirement. 'I am on pension now,' he explained. Was he sad to be going? 'Yes, you get your regulars, it's like a family, you see the same faces, say hello, you know, in the morning. But it's tiring, going up and down those stairs and people, not as friendly as they were, on their phones all the time, wires in their ears.' Did he ever have any problems? 'You tell them,' he said with some vehemence, 'in seven years I never have anyone fall off *my* bus. Well, just one guy,' he added with a beguiling shrug, 'but he was drunk, so that doesn't really count, and he was okay. We cared for our passengers. You tell them.' I shall.

Eleni, a raven-haired Brazilian driver, was sad but sanguine. 'With these new buses, you've got to open the doors, check the passengers are coming on, it's not just driving – but these, these are lovely buses. I'll miss them.' Dave Cook, another driver on route 390, concurred. 'They are lovely buses, they really grip the road. I like driving, it's what I'm good at. I don't want to have to quibble over change and give directions; that's the conductor job. You need the driver to concentrate on the road.' He was retiring too and didn't know quite what he'd do with himself. 'It's wrong, though, isn't it? It's like taking away the red phone boxes or the black taxis, isn't it?'

Across the road the route number and destination blinds on a row of parked 73s began to revolve. I half expected a bell or a cherry to pop into view but the numbers 1, 5 and 9 slotted into place. There was a roar of engines and one by one they drove off, bound for Brixton Garage. 'That's it,' Dave said wearily as he headed back to his cab, 'they won't be heading north again now.'

To a non-participant, bus-spotting gives the impression of being remarkably similar to commuting; mainly a solo activity, unavoidably undertaken in groups. A few of those gathered at the Routemaster farewell knew one another and chatted, swapping information about times and the special models expected – RLW something-or-other was rumoured to be putting in an appearance. Others nodded and glanced at each other, grudging acknowledgements of a familiarity that hours on the kerbside together had produced. Most, however, kept themselves to themselves; the buses were what they were there for, nothing else.

On the edge of the crowd a lanky man with a brown holdall and a distinct shaving nick on his right cheek, a fragment of loo paper stuck to it, was wandering around repeatedly muttering, 'Half the fuckers are on the dole, that's why they're all here today, that's why they're here today,' to no one in particular. It was not clear if he was here for the buses, or was a roving emissary from some New Labour shop-a-scrounger initiative. Everyone ignored him.

The majority of enthusiasts here, laden with camera equipment, were men, but there were one or two doting girlfriends in tow. I tried to approach a thirty-something couple, the woman in Birkenstock sandals and a Union-Jack vest, her partner a bald chap in Gap khakis with modish glasses and a dinky-looking digital camera. He was pogoing around her like Tigger. 'Come on, come on,' he yelled to her as I drew closer. Before I got within spitting distance, they bounced off in the direction of Oxford Street in pursuit of a number 73.

Away from the main huddle, David Kinnear was quietly shooting away. I was initially drawn to him because unlike the others, who kept their lenses firmly trained on the Routemasters (almost as if to glance at another bus would be an act of betrayal punishable by stoning), David was taking pictures of other double deckers as well. 'I like all areas of passenger transport,' he said, excusing what in present company seemed heretically catholic tastes. Buses, it emerged, had been his central passion since he was a child in Dundee, where in the 1980s the local bus company, Stagecoach, used to run a few Routemasters. He said that he came to London from his home in Cambridge about three or four times a year to check out the buses, and thought Transport for London had made 'a tremendous improvement to things'.

On Tyburn Way that evening this was a lonely sentiment. There is always that scene in old horror films when the locals, fed up with whatever mysterious goings-on have been going on up at Castle Aloof-Aristo, suddenly decide that enough is enough and break out the torches. Hearing the name 'Ken Livingstone' echo around here, such a flashpoint occasionally felt only seconds away. 'London without Routemasters just isn't London,' maintained Steve Campbell from Walthamstow, before he launched into a tirade about Ken, Europe and Mercedes Benz, a conspiracy so

Wish you were here: a postcard from the 1960s catches the guardsmen and London's guardsmen red buses on manoeuvres at Wellington Arch.

elaborate that to equal it the mysterious figure on the grassy knoll would have needed to have bumped off both Jack *and* Bobby Kennedy, and then put some time in on Elvis Presley and John Lennon – and nixed Nixon as Deep Throat. 'You tell me,' he said, with the concluding flourish that delusional certainty brings, 'they spent, what, £30,000 refurbishing Routemasters a couple years ago and they're selling them off for £2000 – it doesn't add up.'

Other voices spoke of a loss of civic pride: 'Black cabs, Big Ben and Routemasters, they're icons for London, every one knows that. Can you imagine San Francisco getting rid of its cable cars?' Or the decline of British engineering: 'We used to build our own buses.' Or the effects on tourism: 'Look at the postcards, a lot of them have London buses on and it's not some dull double decker with two doors, it's a Routemaster.'

A 73 drew up, and I decided to head off. I clambered up the stairs and took a seat at the rear of the top deck, to find myself sitting directly behind brown-holdall man. He appeared calmer, quieter – silent actually – inside the bus; the undulation of the engine had soothed him somehow and he clutched the bag under his chin, nuzzling it as you might a lap dog. The seats at the front were exclusively occupied by members of the bus camera-club. Moving along Oxford Street there came a moment when we passed another 73 Routemaster and, like saluting battleships, both top decks exchanged flashbulb fire, to the amusement of passengers who were taking the bus simply to go home. One of them, Annette Croswell, a woman in late middle age and dressed as if she'd wandered out of an early 1970s Gong concert during a pro-tracted flute solo, was no less devoted to the Routemaster. She said she'd lived in Hackney for the past 20 years. 'We don't have the tube, so these buses are really, really important and special to us.' While wholly sympathetic to disabled access and environmental issues, she was not convinced by arguments about safety. 'On these Bendys there's no seats, and on newer double-decker buses people won't go upstairs because it's so hard for them to get off and on, so it's like a cattle truck, people falling all over the place. On the Routemasters people sit down. I know people fall off the back, stupid people, but I think they're much safer. And you've got a conductor, they're reassuring and old people can get some assis-tance. I think it's criminal they're going, I really do.'

There was a man prowling the decks on this bus, an old Gibson

ticket machine strapped to his chest, but he wasn't the real conductor. He was a volunteer, dressed up and helping out for the
day. 'I'm an enthusiast, like yourself,' he said, in his best 'move
along please, there's nothing to see here' tone of voice. A slightly
edgy fellow, with a nest of grey-white hair and glasses whose
lenses could windscreen a Ford Mondeo, he was happy to demon-
strate the ticket machine. 'They're quite weighty,' he said, giving
it a tug and winding the handle to print a ticket out for me. 'You
know, in thirty-seven years' service they only went wrong once.
Marvellous machines. Built to last. Just like the Routemaster.' He
confessed, apropos of nothing, that now he had a girlfriend he
had a lot less spare time for buses. They would, I felt sure, continue to be his first love.

When we reached Albion Parade in Stoke Newington, I hopped
off and crossed over the road for another Routemaster to take me
back to King's Cross. Waiting at the stop were Giles Bowman and
his seven-year-old daughter Charlotte. It was past Charlotte's
bedtime, but Giles was treating her to one final ride on a 73
'before they go all Bendy', as he put it. 'When she was smaller, I
used to tell her red cars were baby Routemasters. It won't be the
same when they've gone.' He looked down at his daughter. 'You'll
be able to say "I remember the 73s in Stoke Newington," won't
you now? Just think, when you're a little old woman, you'll be
able to go "Ooo it was back in September er, er 2004, we had
proper buses then, not like nowadays, Routemasters they were
called."' Charlotte gave her father an indulgent, if slightly with-
ering look as the 73 arrived and we all embarked on our last
journey along Albion Road on a proper bus.

18

AND WHAT DID THE SWISS INVENT?

Among Routemaster enthusiasts, Colin Curtis is the closest thing to a living god. One of the Routemaster's chief engineers, he is to the bus fraternity what Pelé is to football fans or Jimmy Page is to guitar-shop assistants. Buses have been his life, ever since as a small boy growing up in Brighton he was knocked off his bicycle by a Thomas Tilling – 'an ST on route 8,' he recalled. After an apprenticeship at AEC, Curtis joined London Transport as a general technical assistant in September 1947. He was involved with the Routemaster from its inception, working closely on its gearbox, brakes, rear axle and suspension, and although he retired in 1988 he continues to promote his design for a worthy successor, his Q-master bus.

A few days after Black Friday I went to see Curtis at his home near Three Bridges in Sussex, where signs of his vocation were omnipresent. Model buses, immaculate in their cardboard and cellophane packing, cluttered nearly every available surface in the living room, and a large framed colour photograph of a Routemaster occupied the place above the fireplace usually reserved for elaborate mirrors or (once) stuffed animal heads. Milky tea was served, with a wink and a nudge, in London Transport mugs.

Curtis was a ruddy-faced 78-year-old who wore his trousers on the waist. His attitude toward the Routemaster was proud but possibly less sentimental than that of many of its aficionados. 'I think with the RM we had a very versatile vehicle,' he said modestly. 'But,' he added, 'she's fifty years old. The old girl's got to go, I mean we only designed her for seventeen years and with only five or four hundred left they're just not economical to run.'

What irked him was that all the expertise acquired at London Transport through the decades had been cast aside. 'You can't teach experience, you can only learn it. What we had was a perfect set-up. At the workshops we tested everything thoroughly and any problems we dealt with then and there. We had a good relationship with AEC. We could suggest things, and they'd say yes, what a good idea, we'll put that on as standard for you. Now we have buses on chassis again; all the things we sorted out years ago are creeping back in, you see *silly* things . . . like, like windows. On the RM we put the glass in on the inside, you know, like the way you slot lenses into a pair of specs. On too many modern buses they put the window in on the outside. If you've got people fighting on a bus, they brush up against the window and the glass comes straight out, and so do they. You also see little blue lights in the cabs of modern buses. Know why that is? If you look at a Routemaster, the windscreen is at an angle; that stops any reflection. These new things have got decks like Concorde and yet they put a flat windscreen in. The driver can't see the bloody road – only his face. The blue light is there to stop the reflection. It's madness.'

In a conservatory at the back of his house, Curtis gestured to stacks upon stacks of box files, which hold the technical papers he'd rescued from Chiswick's experimental workshop when it closed down. There was more than 30 years' worth of data here on London buses.[68] 'I've got all the records; that stuff out there is copies of all the work, but they just don't want to use it.' He said that essential maintenance equipment from the workshop had been banished to a series of lock-ups, before coming to rest in a railway arch next door to Shepherd's Bush Garage. 'That was how things stood when I left.'

When the topic of the Bendys came up, as it inevitably did, quite what the loss of that kind of corporate knowledge can mean was made apparent. 'Mercedes should have known better than that,' he said expressing undisguised contempt for the working methods of its Mannheim bus plant. 'Those fires[69] should never of happened. We learnt over twenty years ago that to have a short length of pipe between the compressor and the tank, it gets red hot and it sets fire to things. So [he adopted the sing-song cadence of Mr Punch] *what do they do*? Have a shorter length of pipe and lots of wires. It's incredible. I found out later five had caught fire in Germany. The

---

68 Curtis has since donated them to London's Transport Museum.
69 In March 2004, Transport for London operators were forced to withdraw all of their 130-strong fleet of Bendys after the third Bendy in three months burst into flames on Park Lane. (Previous fires had occurred on the Edgware Road and in Camberwell.) The driver and the passengers escaped un-harmed.

design has gone away from the operator to the vehicle builder. I'm sure they work fine in Munich,' he added with a chortle, 'but so they should, we bloody well flattened half of it in the war! The streets of London are a completely different kettle of fish.'

The following week, Curtis appeared at London's Transport Museum in Covent Garden to give a lecture on the Routemaster. The event was a sellout. It was a two-header – a clash of busmen. Curtis was sharing the bill with Andrew Braddock, until recently Head of Access and Mobility at Transport for London. Curtis was up first and led us through the history of the Routemaster, as only he can, with lots of slides and a short film of archive clips – the flickery colour footage of the bus at the 1956 Lord Mayor's Show summoning forth a lost world of hats, pipes and short trousers; all the men looked like George Orwell, while the women had cliffs of hair and unfeasibly pointy breasts. In conclusion, Curtis talked about his Q-master bus. The slide for this unfortunately got jammed in the machine and his finale was drowned in a series of whirrs and clicks as the technician attempted, without success, to retrieve it. The crowd – predominantly gentlemen of a certain age and girth with a fondness for pin-lapel badges – didn't mind and gave him resounding applause.

Next Braddock bounded on to the stage with the ebullience of a Labrador pup chasing a loo roll. From inside his jacket, slowly and theatrically, he drew out a toy Routemaster bus. A delighted 'Ooo' went through the room. 'My God, it's a Triang Spot-On 1/42,' someone announced in a deafening whisper. Braddock smiled, and then retrieved a cigarette lighter from a trouser pocket, its silver glinting under the stage lights. Holding both aloft, he sparked up the lighter with a resonant *ping* and set fire to the bus. 'The Routemaster is a flaming fiery roll of death,' he bellowed, waving the blazing toy before him. The audience gasped. A woman in the front row fainted. 'You unfeeling monster,' cried an elderly man, comforting a small woman whimpering next to him, possibly his wife.

No, Braddock didn't do any of this, and no one fainted, but it was close. Braddock enjoyed his role as the joke-cracking, power-point-wielding nemesis, and he was good at it. 'The Routemaster was out of date before it was built,' he said. The open platform was 'a conflict zone'; bus conductors were 'lazy'. On the screen behind him flow charts and diagrams of what he referred to as 'people movers for a modern city' danced into view, as he spoke about 'halving the number of bus stops', 'importing tube values' and adding 'a good continental flavour to the capital's buses'. He finished and the claps, timorous to begin with, soon grew deafening in nervous overcompensation.

Curtis returned to the stage, and a woman from the museum called for questions from the floor. There had been plenty to chew over: Braddock had spent around 20 minutes repeatedly punching in the face what for the majority was an old and faithful friend, and it took a while before the first hand was raised. 'Yes, you sir, in the brown jacket,' the woman said to the lone arm in the centre. 'What is the weight of the Routemaster?' a voice asked, to a murmur of relief.

'It should never have been built. It should never really have been contemplated,' Braddock reiterated on the telephone a couple of days later. 'As long as we hung on to this anarchic idea that a bus rolls along the streets with no doors, with people getting on and off at will, very unsafely be it noted,[70] then we were never going to get anywhere. We've got to sweep away some of these emotions. It's a 1912 design, front-engine, open rear-platform bus – bloody dangerous and well past its sell-by date. I know it makes me an absolute heretic to be strung up and hung, drawn and quartered but I really do believe what I say.'

I liked Braddock; he was sharp and funny. But, unsurprisingly, we butted heads like a couple of rams. He said that you never saw Bendys bunching because they had predictable boarding

---

70   There was 'an average' of two deaths a year on Routemasters. The last was recorded in December 2004, when a 41-year-old woman fell off the number 19 on Upper Street, Islington, hitting her head on the pavement.

times; that conductors were unaffordable, never went upstairs and never gave passengers the right information; that Routemasters were not as iconic as San Francisco's cable cars. I countered with tales of Bendy bus logjams in Stoke Newington; recalled a very recent example of a conductor striding about on the upper deck of a 38 dispensing information to Spanish tourists about how to get to Covent Garden from Charing Cross Road. And San Francisco, icons?

'I really just don't happen to think it is as historically important or iconic as the cable cars in San Francisco. If you've been to San Francisco and *understand* the cable cars, they are absolutely and totally unique. Of course, the RM is an icon, but the RT was an icon. Any bus which is quirky and old is iconic, especially in a country which is obsessed with its history and its empire and has no real idea of its place in the modern world and its place in Europe.'

Braddock put me in mind, in some respects, of a Europhile variant of what Tom Wolfe once called 'the Mid-Atlantic Man'. He uses phrases like 'way more' and, in reference to one-person operation, said 'we self-inflicted'. He spoke of himself as 'a European first and an Englishman second'. Here was a man who had strolled down those Boulevards, the Vias and Strasses, tasted the coffee, maybe nibbled a little strudel and watched in awe as his fellow Europeans marched, neatly, efficiently, on to immaculate 18-metre articulated buses that arrived on time. He returned to Britain with a vision of a better way, a way more way – the Swiss way, apparently. And in this, perhaps, he's no different from George Shillibeer. His advocacy of the Bendys may be vindicated in the long run. (A 'Walk', a 'Way' or a 'Way More' will be named in his honour.) 'You have to ask the serious question,' he said at one point, 'why is it that the good old double decker only exists in Britain and not in the rest of Europe? Can it really be the *Daily Mail* idea that we are right and they are wrong?'

To which my response was, *vive la différence*. I was reminded of the French film *Un Air de Famille*, in which the owner of a café woos back his estranged wife by promising to convert the business into an English-style pub. Oh, how people guffawed in the Everyman cinema in Hampstead when that came up. Why would anyone want to turn their lovely café into a mundane old pub? What we admire about many European capital cities is their ability to hang on to their traditions, their proper shops and local cafés etc etc. Yes, okay, and their adequately funded public transport systems. But we in McLondonbucks, if nothing else, at least had our crap pubs and proper buses with conductors. London, despite self-abasing plans to turn Oxford Street into a continental piazza and unleash 24-hour café-style drinking, is not Paris, Munich or Zurich. London is a greater assimilator, arguably the most successful multicultural city in the world. A world city. Lucerne, while no doubt a lovely place, isn't. The Swiss, those pioneers of cashless bus travel systems in the 1960s according to Braddock, did not give women the vote until 1971. It is currently illegal to mow your front lawn dressed as Elvis in Switzerland. Famously, it took the English to conquer the Alps.[71]

I realize I sound like Harry Lime – that business about the cuckoo clock – but you don't have to be a Little Englander to feel

---

71   The term 'alpes' was used to describe the high-level pastures used for grazing. The locals had no name for the mountains themselves.

that something distinctive, significant, is being lost with the passing of the Routemaster; or aggrieved by the inadequacy of anything as stylish, indigenous even, to replace it.

I suggested to Braddock that this really was the crux of the problem, that change would be easier to embrace if a new London bus, like the newer black cabs or the new Minis and MGs, took design cues from its forebears. A future-retro bus that could be as desirable as, say, a Smart Car, and fill the gaping void in the capital's landscape left by the Routemaster's demise.

'I wouldn't disagree with that – I have a Smart Car myself – but in the cold hard light of day, I don't think it would increase the number of passengers or get people out of their cars. Certain people may go "oh that's a nice piece of design" . . . but the majority of people just get on the first bus that comes along and don't really give a bugger what colour it is.'

It may have been static on the line but I was sure, just then, that I heard Frank Pick turning in his grave.

19

A BUS OF OUR OWN

'The big thing,' Sue Dobbing said, 'is to go from not owning to owning.' Dobbing spoke as we sat inside the Routemaster that she and her husband Chris, a GP, had only recently purchased. Chris, Sue said, had driven their bus here – to the Routemaster 50th rally in Finsbury Park – after a single hour's lesson. She sounded both genuinely proud and genuinely flabbergasted. Chris acknowledged the compliment/possible insult with an equally ambiguous shake of his head.

A Routemaster is, obviously, a big thing to own. They are not by current standards especially expensive to buy – not for something the size of a small house. Since what is known as 'volume sales' (a polite euphemism for the stripping of the altars, as far as many Londoners are concerned) began again in August 2003,

Routemasters have been changing hands for between
£5000–£10,000 depending on the condition. If you are lucky, or
fancy a challenge, shabbier models can be picked up for about
£2000. A new Mini, by comparison, costs more than £14,000, a
vintage Morris Minor about £2500. They are big, difficult to
garage, and at 8 miles to the gallon, rather a pricey run-around for
trips to the shops.[72]

Sue wasn't entirely sure what they were going to do with
theirs. 'We may convert the top, we just don't know yet. We may
end up buying another one.' This seemed an interesting solution
to the problem – an instance of, as the joke has it, a problem
shared is a problem that two people have; a problem two people
with two buses have. But Jane Barton, her friend and the co-
owner of RM1471 for the past decade, assured me that 'sticking
to one, was really, really difficult'. They made it sound like one of
those 'swift halfs' after work that wind up in the wee small hours
of the morning in a Spanish bar on Hanway Street. One more for
the road, anyone?

In his essay *The Lion and the Unicorn* (1941), George Orwell
defined the English as a 'nation of stamp-collectors . . . coupon-
snippers, darts-players, crossword-puzzle fans'. Sue and Jane both
cast Routemaster ownership in this proud tradition of mild-
mannered, noun-verb, English eccentricity. 'I do think you have to
be slightly unconventional to carry it off. Having a big red bus is
a big statement, and you get lots of attention. It's completely

---

72 More economical, nonetheless, than any of the buses which are replacing them
    which manage a pitiful 5½ miles to the gallon. (*Evening Standard* 27 July
    2004)

harmless though,' Jane said. Sue added, 'If anyone heard you were buying a canal boat, they'd say "wow" but what's the difference? I don't think it's any stranger to buy a bus.'

Canal boats, I suspected, were usually purchased to live on – the gentrifying middle classes, never slow to colonize redundant industrial spaces (warehouses, factories, power stations, public toilets), hadn't as yet reconciled themselves to semi-immobile mobile homes. The phrase 'trailer park', usually combined with that other American import 'white trash', drained the concept of any residual romantic associations with country lanes, travelling tinkers and painted Roma wagons.

Jane and her partner, Ian Rushby, were on this occasion busless owing to a blown gasket; the only major problem they'd ever had with their bus, she insisted. Patrons of Jacqueline's Discotheque in Wardour Street at the fag end of the 1980s

might well recall Jane's and Ian's Routemaster. Painted pink in those days, it was the club's courtesy bus. Subsequently converted into a mobile home, it had been Rushby's *pied-à-terre* when the couple met.

'I was a Londoner for nearly thirty years and used the Routemasters every day, and then moved away. And then there was Ian, living on one,' Jane said. 'It's a nostalgia thing, but still to this day when I walk up the stairs in my own bus to go to bed it taps into something, the memories, it reminds me of being a child.' Sue believed it affected her husband in much the same way. 'As a child,' she said, 'Chris used to take his sisters around London on the buses, so they were totally a part of his childhood.'

As I discovered from Steve Newman of Ensign Buses, Jane (and Chris) are far from the only owners in search of lost childhoods (*A la recherche du Routemaster perdu*). A family firm based in Purfleet, Essex, Ensign has spent a quarter of a century raising old London buses from the dead, buying up fleets of unwanted models and selling them on to operators, collectors and preservationists across the globe. More than 400 of the last London Routemasters will be sold through the company – some becoming cherished pets of doting individuals,[73] others getting new identities as television and film props, open-top sightseers, bars and restaurants and, most depressingly of all, estate agents' offices.[74]

---

73 Including the odd celeb. Natalie Appleton, the former All Saint, purchased a Routemaster from Ensign as a gift for her husband Liam Howlett of the dance act The Prodigy. He is the quiet, brooding power behind the synthesizer rather than the one with the Shockheaded Peter hair, piercings and tattoos who used to do all the shouting.

74 Can't they leave their hands off anything?

I asked Steve what the main reason people gave for wanting to buy a Routemaster was. 'Travelling on them as a kid,' he replied with no hesitation. (Show me the child at five on the 113 to Apex Corner and I'll show you the Routemaster owner.) But was that all? Just nostalgia? When London Regional Transport began to put its surplus stocks of Routemasters up for sale in February 1985, *Punch* advised its readers to: 'Buy yours now . . . We suspect these buses to be a good investment. Quite apart from their intrinsic pleasing character, do we not know from experience that, before very long, there will be government directives and EEC initiatives decreeing the abolition of the OPO [one-person operation] and the introduction of a pioneering new concept in transport? This will be a bus operated by two people, with an open platform at the back and it will look exactly like the Routemaster. There can be no doubt.'

Fat chance, but I found it difficult to believe that in the course of the intervening 20 years people had become any less interested in investments – in 1985 there were people, not many admittedly, who continued to think of a house as something you could live *in* rather than *off*. 'I am sure that's a part of it,' said Steve. 'I do tell people that if you follow its predecessor, the RT – and there were seven thousand of them built – well, they used to go for eight hundred to a thousand pounds. A decent one in good condition, licensed for the road, will set you back a minimum of fifteen grand now.'

Graham Lunn, secretary and one of the founders of the Routemaster Association, was more sceptical about the financial returns on a Routemaster. 'You never get your money back. You never get back what you have to spend on them to keep them

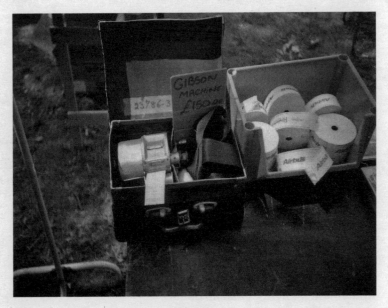

going,' he said with a smidgen of pride. Lunn is a bus driver.[75] He drove Routemasters on the 13 route from Golders Green to the Aldwych for London Transport in the 1990s. He's owned a Routemaster since 1983. Buses were merely a hobby when he bought his Routemaster. He took that fateful step of turning what was once a pastime into a career – an ambition nursed at heart by many a hobbyist but usually resisted on the grounds that the frisson could wear off if it became just a job. Nowadays, as he drives

---

75   According to Brewer's *Dictionary of Phrase and Fable*, there was once upon a time, in the days of the horse bus, a bus driver who spent his holiday travelling to and fro on a bus driven by his chums. The story is said to have given rise to the phrase 'a busman's holiday' for any activity done in spare time that is dangerously close to work.

buses outside the capital, the distinction between business and pleasure is easier for Lunn to maintain. 'My other bus,' he can tell his regular passengers, 'is a Routemaster.'

Lunn said that bus preservationists – and especially Routemaster owners – have traditionally been drawn from within the industry. They tended to be engineers, mechanics, garage staff, drivers, conductors; people who had always hankered after a bus to call their own. This older group of preservationists have been dying out in recent years. Preservation and simply what you *do* with a bus had, he said, 'been getting more and more difficult'. He feared that preservation was in terminal decline. 'It isn't what it used to be. If you go to as many bus shows as us, well, you see that the age group, well, it's not as young as it should be, and the shows, they are beginning to dwindle.'

Punch, it turned out, had been on the money in one respect. In 2000, when Transport for London was clamouring out for Routemasters to refurbish and redeploy on the capital's streets, Lunn said, quite a few of the association's longest-standing members had sold their buses back into service. 'Some of them were getting on a bit, didn't want the hassle any more and they thought at that time it was a fair price.' (Lunn was approached but told them to 'naff off, in the politest possible way'.)

I was sure Lunn was right. Bus preservation probably wasn't what it had been. But what was it becoming? Would there be any buses in the future people actually wanted to preserve? The demise of the Routemaster, oh bitter irony, had, of course, revived interest in old buses and, as Lunn conceded, infused their association with new owners and plenty of fresh blood. Steve from Ensign told me that they had interest from people 'who'd never

ever thought of buying a bus before'. People, I surmised maybe unfairly, a little like Sue and Chris. They were joiners-in, paid-up members; happy, it appeared, to be a part of the scene. Not all of these newer owners, it struck me, would crave the camaraderie of the shows – and certainly not in quite the same way that those who had once worked for large, paternalistic organizations such as London Transport might have done . . .

Neither Jane nor Sue was a London resident, living in Lincolnshire and Peterborough respectively. I was intrigued to know what they thought about the Routemasters' removal from London. Jane said it was a shame; Sue expressed some sadness but was unflinchingly pragmatic. 'I would like to see one or two routes running, as they are part of the history of London, and a very well-designed part of that history. I wish the same design, the same thought went into other things, but the reality is they were built for a purpose but they are not fulfilling that purpose any more. They don't have access to all, the disabled can't get aboard. We do,' she continued, addressing me gravely, 'have to think seriously about emissions.'

I agreed (who wouldn't?) but in 2000 the refitted Routemasters with their Cummins engines were among the greenest buses in London. In any case, I wondered how they squared their bus ownership with what were obviously heartfelt concerns about the environment. 'Our bus is our holiday home, has been for the last seven years,' Jane said. 'We don't do flying holidays which are much more harmful to the planet, so ethically I think we are okay.'

Over the course of the conversation it emerged that Jane's partner, Ian, hadn't travelled on a Routemaster bus in London until this year. Catching up with him later on, I wanted to know why, free of any of the typical London or nostalgic associations, he'd bought it. 'I first came across the bus when I was looking for a home,' he said. 'It was around the time that new age travellers were Thatcher's new enemy within and so I was worried about having something too provocative. I had friends who lived in ambulances and in old buses. I thought with this Routemaster, it still looks decent, like a big smiley London bus from the outside.' It was precisely the bus's 'big smiley' design that had encouraged him in July 2001 to drive it to the G8 Summit in Genoa to promote the Drop the Debt Campaign. 'When we went to the G8, it was with a Christian group from Leeds,' he explained. 'We were going to somewhere where violence seemed quite likely and they wanted something that looked as friendly and non-threatening as possible.'

The Routemaster had represented a 'benign Britishness'; a Britain of free speech, democracy, integrity and fair play (and amusingly antiquated transport facilities? A spent industrial power who hadn't built anything good for 20 years?). Whatever it was, it was a Britain, an England, comfortable with itself, its moral centre intact. (Orwell's England again, perhaps? 'A land where the bus conductors are good-tempered and the policemen carry no revolvers.')[76]

Ian managed to imbue his bus with an organic quality; he spoke of it in terms of a yearly cycle. Each autumn the bus was lagged and packed away for the winter, and revived again each spring when 'crackpot plans were hatched' and trips to

---

76 *England, Your England,* from *The Lion and the Unicorn* (1941). Nothing is

Glastonbury and a bus-bound summer holiday in Europe arranged. In Lincolnshire, it seemed, this Routemaster, once so calibrated to the rhythms of London life, had gone entirely rustic. It was dignified old age.

Wandering around Finsbury Park that afternoon, I realized, in retrospect, how much the Routemaster rally had stirred memories of the agricultural shows I'd been dragged to as a child. Amid the pens of animals and the trestle tables flogging jam, there'd always been one or two or three old steam traction engines pottering around. Relics of bygone eras. Lined up smartly in Finsbury Park, the Routemasters gave off a similar aura. From now on, or very soon, everything would be re-enactment – 'The Sealed Knot' meets *Summer Holiday*; a pastiche, the Routemaster wheeled out in London like the proverbial (because rarely seen) pearly kings and queens.

What did Steve, someone who had grown up quite literally surrounded by old buses, make of it all? 'If they were buildings,' he said, 'they'd be listed.' He added, 'It's a great, great shame. The Routemaster is a brand and the end of ninety years of that style of bus. Terrible shame, and the end of an era.'

---

value-free, except nothing itself that is, and in April 2005, the UUP launched their election campaign in Northern Ireland with a Routemaster bus – the destination blind set for 'Westminster'.

20

TERMINUS

The Routemaster's active life in London is at its end.[77] It has had a good innings – Denis Compton, to pursue the metaphor, was in his final season for England when it first appeared on the capital's streets. Isn't it time to move on? London buses are, after all, 'now carrying the highest number of passengers since 1969'. By the autumn of 2005 every London bus *should* be fully accessible. It would be churlish, offensive even, to suggest that these were, in

---

77 On the issue of Heritage Routes, at the People's Question Time at the Mermaid Theatre on 2 March 2004, London Mayor Ken Livingstone said: 'We are going to keep some, like San Francisco kept its cable cars. There will be a route going around the main tourist attractions of Central London and anyone with an Oyster card will be able to hop on and off and so on; they won't be like the present tourist buses.' Six central routes, operated by 50 of the greenest re-engined buses, had originally been mooted.

principle, anything but good things. In a customer survey comparing the Routemasters on route 36 with the Bendys on the parallel route 436 during the spring of 2003, 'the vast majority of passengers on articulated buses . . . considered the new service to be superior.' And yet . . . and yet.

What are we losing? What have we lost?

The Routemaster was not just any old bus.[78] It is/was, to quote the Westminster council leader, Simon Milton, 'very much part of London's brand. It is what visitors expect.'

Brand: an overused and irritating word, I know, but you get the point. Mess with 'the brand' at your peril. If it were a building, as Steve Newman from Ensign noted, it would be listed. London devoid of Routemasters is, to pinch the title of Geoffrey Fletcher's classic book, the London That Nobody Knows. I am perfectly aware that London was once a city of trams, trolleybuses, RT buses, horse buses, lamplighters, lethal peasoupers, open sewers and public hangings, and that it survived those losses. Samuel Johnson railed against 'the fury of innovation' and complained that 'the age is running mad after change' upon learning that public processions from Newgate Gaol to the gallows at Tyburn were to be swept away. We

---

78 Due to their extensive regular overhauls and major refurbishments in the 1990s and in 2000, their age is deceptive. Rather like the Ship of Theseus, where over time every single plank had been replaced, only the outer bodywork on some of these last models is, as it were, 'old'. In 2004 one of Transport for London's chief engineers pronounced them mechanically sound for a further ten years. However, under TfL's proposed Low Emissions Zone, due to come into force by 2007, only the last 50 Routemasters refitted with the 'greener' Cummins engines would meet its conditions.

coped without them. As A N Wilson observed in the introduction to his *Faber Book of London* (1993), a Routemaster-free
volume, I am afraid to report,[79] 'fings ain't wot they used to be'
has been an abiding preoccupation of London literature
through the centuries. Cities do get better and worse, declining
and falling in several famous instances. The ones that thrive are
those that adapt and move on. ('If you want things to stay the
same,' as a character in Lampedusa's novel *The Leopard* says,
'they are going to have to change.') London is, as is repeated to
the point of tediousness, an adapter. But we can't pretend that
there aren't consequences or that 'progress' shouldn't be tem-
pered where necessary by a respect for the past.

The Routemaster was made to measure, Savile Row tailored for
the city; 'an attractive piece of street furniture' specifically built
for London. It exemplified the highest ideals of a public-spirited
passenger transport service – physical evidence that London and
ordinary Londoners should have the very best. 'A handsome city

---

79   London buses are not overlooked but two pieces where buses feature promi-
     nently (an extract from D H Lawrence's essay *Dull London* and Rudyard Kipling's
     poem *In Partibus*) are located in the *Hating It* section of the book. The opening
     stanza of Kipling's 1889 poem, a characteristically little drummer boy effort, writ-
     ten shortly after he arrived in the capital from India in October 1889, runs:

>   *The 'buses run to Battersea,*
>   *The 'buses run to Bow,*
>   *The 'buses run to Westbourne Grove,*
>   *And Notting Hill also;*
>   *But I am sick of London Town*
>   *From Shepherd's Bush to Bow.*

deserves a handsome transport,' as *All That Mighty Heart*, the London Transport film, proclaimed in 1962. We loved it, not because it was old and quirky, but because it was bloody good. Well made ('fit for its purpose' in Frank Pick's phrase). Importantly, it greeted us as an equal. It respected our custom. It was comfortable. Convenient. Efficient. We were free to get on and get off, within reason, when we wanted to. 'Passengers,' an old London Transport motto maintained, 'are our business not an interruption to our service.' And on a Routemaster you could believe in that too.

Of course, it grew out of and was born into another world. The society it was created to serve was more, or more visibly, stratified. It was a world with a certain intolerance of difference; you might see in its straight rows of seats a reflection of the rigidity of those times. A bus built for a city known for forming orderly queues

rather than for wild alcoholic sprees; for a city of parsimonious coupon-snippers rather than designer-label consumers. It's a bus that can exclude (the disabled, the pushchair), I concede. I prefer, however, to see a more egalitarian spirit at work. It was designed for (nearly) everyone, and everyone aboard is equal. By its careful, skilful design, it was intended in some small way to elevate an everyday experience.

By contrast, the metaphors many modern buses offer are slightly depressing. Their designs indicate troubled minds: seats on different levels, seats back to front, lurid playpen fabrics and colour schemes, straps at unusable heights, lava-lamp globules of extruded plastic at every turn and a soundtrack of bleeps and ticks. The Bendys have all the aesthetics of the inside of a Hoover

A new block on the block: ugly, boxy, bulky;
the shape of London buses since the 1970s.

attachment. New double deckers are huge, boxy, noisy and
unwieldy. They look deformed, bulked out, like Action Man after
Hasbro pumped him full of steroids and turned him into some
kind of inhuman gym-bunny cyberpunk in the 1990s. The average speed of a London bus continues to hover around 11 mph,
and yet the engines on these vehicles seem tuned to accelerate
with a speed and abruptness previously reserved for propelling
dogs into space.

They are usually standard models bought off-the-shelf from
large multinational manufacturers (Mercedes-Benz-Daimler,
Volvo, DAF) and as homogenized and bland as a Gap T-shirt. If
London's overriding purpose is to provide ever more convenient
chainstore shopping, then perhaps these buses match that aspi-
ration perfectly. Perhaps we are getting the buses we deserve, the
buses we want.[80]

When my father was courting my mother, he would often go
round to her house for tea. Out of politeness, he'd refuse any
second helpings – additional slices of Battenberg, more cups of
Tetley – saying that he'd had 'Ample, thanks'. He was known as
'Ample Thanks' on my mother's side of the family for the next

---

80 This is certainly what Ken Livingstone and Transport for London would have
    us believe. Again on 3 March 2004, Ken said: 'When I was more able to run
    and jump on and off the back of Routemasters I thought they were wonder-
    ful too. Now I sometimes struggle with a child or a lot of shopping, and I have
    to say they are nothing like as friendly as I remember them. Whether you like
    it or not, all our surveys do show that the single most popular bus we've got
    is the Bendy bus . . . All over, people are saying they would like the Bendy
    buses in their area. I will come back and look at the issue of whether we could
    increase the number of seats on the Bendy bus.'

20 years. I mention this because the end of the Routemaster, it seems to me, has also called time on the notion of a full bus. With no conductors, and drivers having far less control over how many people board their buses, we squeeze ourselves aboard, no matter how full a bus is. Buses designed to make standing the norm (the Bendys have space for 91 standees) encourage us in the belief that 'one more on' won't make any difference. A bigger bus can mean a less frequent bus, and that makes us less enthusiastic about waiting for the next one. We'd rather get aboard now and get the whole damned thing over with.

The Bendy has been nicknamed the 'happy bus', the 'free bus' and on route 73 the 'seventy-free', because of the ease with which fares can be evaded. This was illustrated in November 2004 when an *Evening Standard* journalist spent 10 hours on the 'seventy-free' without once having to show his ticket. At the time, TfL claimed that its survey showed fare evasion on all routes was 'only 2.2 per cent' and it was lower on Bendy buses, at '2.1 per cent'.

However, in January 2005, five 'revenue inspectors' were suspended for refusing to collect fares on the Bendys, claiming that the job had become too dangerous. 'You get an army of people who just refuse to pay. You ask them for their ticket and they just look at you and say "Fuck off, it's a free bus",' one of the suspended inspectors told the *Evening Standard*.

When I started writing this book I was living in Tufnell Park, in a flat bang opposite the tube. Hulking, oversized, overfed double-decker buses on route 134 to Archway drove past our kitchen window every hour of the day, creating a thrum and hiss that was

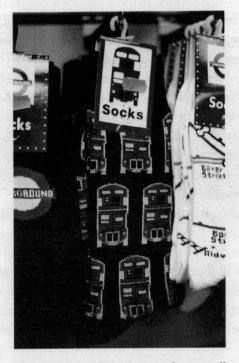

impossible to ignore. Around the corner, fractionally out of view
and completely out of earshot, the 390 Routemasters ploughed
back and forth to King's Cross, in their own quietly efficient and
self-effacing way. Most mornings, I used to catch one down to the
British Library near St Pancras, savouring the pleasures of the ride,
before spending the day browsing self-published pamphlets on
the Greenline services in the 1960s.

On my walk to the bus stop, I'd usually see an elderly derelict,
his hands always encased in oversized industrial rubber gloves,
clinging on to the railings near the Spaghetti House Restaurant on
the corner of Fortess Road. Ahab on the slipstreams of the A1, his

mornings were devoted to staring at the flows of traffic that passed before him. Usually a sage-like observer, indifferent to the sirens, beeping horns and screeching tyres, he would intermittently be roused into rage by particular vehicles. Refuse lorries caused him no end of dismay.

Later in the year I moved to Stoke Newington, but a few weeks afterwards I had to return to the old flat to pick up some post. Coming out of the tube on a grey autumn afternoon, I found Old Rubber Gloves was still there; this time howling like a banshee at a brand-new double decker on route 390. He sounded as if he was in pain, but then he'd always sounded that way. It's easy, perhaps, to read too much into these things.

21

9 DECEMBER, 2005

It was time to catch the last bus. Questions had been raised in Parliament. A petition had been signed by 10,000 people. Reams of newspaper column inches and an *Evening Standard* campaign were devoted to its preservation. A poll commissioned by the think tank Policy Exchange reported that 81 per cent of people opposed its scrapping. Internet message boards and radio phone-ins had been filled with impassioned Routemaster-related chatter. But as summer replaced autumn and Cliff Richard vowed never to record again, Routemasters had dwindled to a single working route in the city. Then the last day arrived. RM2117 was scheduled to embark on the final journey from Marble Arch to Streatham on Route 159 at 12.10pm on Friday, 9 December, 2005 – two months shy of the 50th anniversary of the Routemaster's maiden passenger voyage. But after nearly half a century it was in no obvious hurry to depart.

All around the western end of Oxford Street mourners lined the pavements. Bus enthusiasts – notebooks, printed schedules and cameras in hand – and ordinary Londoners stood side by side, their ranks swollen by the police, television teams, press photographers, bemused Christmas shoppers, and a small contingent of disabled-rights campaigners bearing placards with the slogans 'The End is Nigh' and 'Good Riddance to the Routemaster' written on them. It was bitterly cold and foggy. London weather circa 1962 seemed to have been hired especially for the occasion. And as the deadline passed and Routemasters continued to trundle along, people started to grow restless. Where was the last bus? Was this one it? Or that one? When would it all end, exactly? For a while no one was quite sure.

At about 12.20, a gold-painted Routemaster pulled up at the

stop. 'Is that the last one? A bling bus?' a woman asked, audibly distressed. 'No, it can't be. Not a gold one, that would be wrong. They wouldn't have a gold one as the last one *would they?*' her male companion replied uncertainly. Lingering doubts were soon quashed when a man with unruly grey hair turned to them and helpfully chipped in. 'No, this is RM6. The last one's RM2117'. The couple beamed back at him, gratitude and mild incomprehension combining in their smiles. Whatever bus gobbledegook this was didn't matter today – would undoubtedly never matter to them again. For the moment they were happy. The last Routemaster would not, at least, be gold.

The minutes ticked on. A middle-aged man with a moustache, wearing a college scarf, began berating the disabled protesters. Pirouetting on the toes of his brogues, and jabbing a finger in the direction of a woman in a wheelchair, he unleashed a stream of bile. 'You've got your way; take your sign away. You people are stupid. You people are pathetic.' Not unreasonably, they pointed out that it was a free country and that all they were fighting for was a more inclusive society, but he refused to be pacified. Any semblance of a civilised debate finally gave way when, in a wild breach of logic, he yelled, 'You want to stop people playing football.' None of the disabled protesters could recall that football had even been mentioned until then.

When RM2117 finally arrived, a lightening storm of flashbulbs exploded and an elderly man in an electric wheelchair was gently persuaded by a policeman to abandon an attempt to block its path. In what felt like a few seconds the passengers had scrambled aboard and the Routemaster was off, pursued by a big open-topped media bus. As it rumbled down the street after its quarry, with boom microphones and cameras sprouting everywhere, it resembled a harpoon-pronged Moby Dick bearing down on the Pequod.

In the weeks that followed the Routemaster would glide across the nation's television screens in the Christmas Day episode of Doctor Who; be voted, along with the cup of tea, an official Icon of England, and nominated to compete against other totems of our industrial decline, Concorde and the Chopper bicycle, in something called The Great British Design Quest. But in London it was a phantom omnibus, a ghost of Oxford Street haunting the city. Eight survive on the 'heritage routes', but they are gone by dusk and, like cabbies, not seen south of the river. To hop on one now is to take a journey into the day before yesterday, which is history.

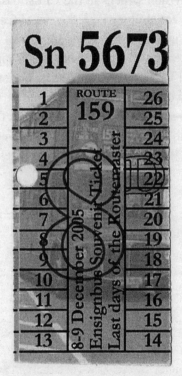

Sn 5673

1	ROUTE	26
2	**159**	25
3		24
4		23
5		22
6		21
7		20
8		19
9		18
10		17
11		16
12		15
13		14

8-9 December 2005
Ensignbus Souvenir Ticket
Last days of the Routemaster

Appendix 1

SOME DATES

1829 George Shillibeer brings a Parisian-style omnibus to London, operating a passenger service from Paddington to Bank.

1856 The Anglo-French London General Omnibus Company is formed.

1908 The General takes over both Vanguard and the London Road Car Company – becoming the dominant bus company in London.
      A separate subsidiary coach-building company based at the Vanguard's old works in Walthamstow, called the Associated Equipment Company (AEC), is formed.

1910 The General and its new subsidiary, AEC, build the first mass production motorbus – the B-type bus, 'Old Bill'.

1911 The General runs its last horse bus in London.

1912 The General Omnibus Company becomes part of the Underground Group.

1914– During the First World War, more than 1000 London
1918   General B-type buses are used as troop carriers in
        Flanders and France.

1922   The London General opens its overhaul works on a 31-
        acre site off Chiswick High Road.

1925   The General sets up a training centre for drivers and
        conductors at Chiswick.
        London General brings the first roofed double
        deckers – the NS class – to London.

1927   AEC's new factory in Southall is opened.

1930   The General establishes a subsidiary, Greenline, to run
        suburban routes.

1932   Harry Beck's diagrammatic tube map is adopted by the
        Underground.

1933   The London Passenger Transport Act establishes the
        London Transport Passenger Board – the largest
        passenger operating organization in the world.
        Baron Ashfield and Frank Pick are appointed Chairman
        and Chief Executive of the board.
        The London General is subsumed in London Transport.

1939– The first RT buses – the Routemasters' predecessors –
1945   appear in 1939 but production is stopped by the
        outbreak of the Second World War.
        Chiswick works is turned over to aircraft production.

1947   Discussions about a new chassis-less aluminium bus for
        London begin at London Transport.
        The first post-war RT buses go into service.

1948   The British Transport Commission is established and
        brings London Transport under national ownership.

1949   London buses acquire a former tube depot at
        Aldenham in Hertfordshire for a new central overhaul
        works.

1950   The withdrawal of London's trams begins.

1951   A new, government-appointed London Transport
        Executive is founded, positioning London Transport
        rather awkwardly between the government and the
        British Transport Commission.

1952   The last tram runs in London from Woolwich to New
        Cross on 5 July.
        Plans for the Routemaster bus, then coded IM, are
        finalized and the designer Douglas Scott is employed
        to assist with the design.
        A deal is arranged for AEC and Park Royal Vehicles to
        build the first prototype.

1954   London Transport announces it will withdraw the
        trolleybuses – a new diesel double-decker bus will
        replace them.
        London's 'Bus of the Future' – RM1, the first
        prototype of the Routemaster – is unveiled at the
        Commercial Motor Show in Earl's Court.

1955   The second prototype Routemaster RM2 is built.

1956   The Routemaster (RM1) makes its maiden passenger
        voyage on Route 2 from Golders Green station to
        Crystal Palace.

1957   Two further prototype Routemasters are built: RML3
        is engined by Leyland with a body by Weymann (the
        L in the code standing for Leyland); CRL4 also has a
        Leyland engine but a body by Eastern Coach Works.

1958   A bus strike lasts for two months.
       The first 'production' Routemaster built by AEC and
       Park Royal vehicles is completed.
1959   Full-scale production of Routemasters gets underway
       at AEC and Park Royal in September.
1960   Traffic wardens are deployed in London for the first
       time.
1961   The first of a longer type of Routemaster (RML) with
       72 seats is built. An unpainted aluminium Routemaster
       nicknamed the 'Silver Lady' hits the capital's streets.
1962   The Transport Act 1962 abolishes the British Transport
       Commission, creating a new London Transport Board,
       directly responsible to the Minister for Transport. The
       last trolleybus runs in London from Wimbledon to
       Fulwell.
       AEC and Park Royal become part of the Leyland
       Motor Group.
1963   The Cliff Richard musical movie *Summer Holiday* goes
       on general release.
       The first Beatles album appears.
       Sexual intercourse begins.
1964   Corgi and Dinky both release toy Routemaster buses.
       The Phelps Brown Report on bus workers' pay and
       conditions is published.
1965   London Transport begins trials with Daimler Fleetline
       and Leyland Atlantean double-decker buses.
       Barbara Castle becomes Minister for Transport.
       The Greater London Council is established.
1966   *Time* magazine declares London 'the Swinging City'.

London Transport announces its plans to press on with its 'one-man bus operation' and starts to operate single-decker Merlin Buses on a Red Arrow express route between Victoria and Marble Arch.

1967   Barbara Castle negotiates the transfer of control of London Transport to the Greater London Council.

1968   The last Routemaster to be built – RML2760 – leaves Park Royal's factory in March.
Barbara Castle's Transport Act creating a National Bus Company and legalizing one-man double-decker bus operation comes into force.

1969   The first Routemaster to endure an all-over advertising paint job appears.

1970   The Greenline and Country bus services pass into the hands of a new subsidiary of the National Bus Company, London Country Bus Services Ltd.

1977   London Transport starts to buy back some Routemasters from the country areas and begins to redeploy them on central London routes.

1979   The RT bus – after 40 years' service – leaves the capital. The first Daimler DMS buses – the intended replacements for the Routemasters – are withdrawn from service.
British Leyland closes AEC's Southall factory.

1981   Park Royal folds amid the economic downturn.
Ken Livingstone and Labour gain control of the GLC, and bring in a Fares Fair policy, raising rates to reduce fares, to encourage public transport use. It draws a legal challenge from the Conservative borough of Bromley.

London Transport abandons plans for its new London double decker.

1982   The House of Lords rules the GLC Fares Fair policy unlawful.

The first mass withdrawals of Routemaster in London commence, and continue through the decade.

1984   London Regional Transport is created, bringing the reign of the London Transport Executive to an end as the service is primed for privatization.

1986   Aldenham bus works closes in November.

The GLC is abolished.

Privatized and deregulated bus companies in the provinces start to buy up Routemasters and employ them in the regions.

1988   Partial deregulation brings competitive tendering to central London, with the result that the Grey-Green Company runs grey and green liveried buses on route 24 through Parliament Square.

1990   Routemaster withdrawals dwindle and a series of refurbishments commence – a fleet of just over 600 Routemasters remains in London.

Chiswick works closes.

1991   Smoking is banned on all London buses.

1992–   Most of London's Routemasters are extensively
1994   refurbished and new Iveco or Cummins engines installed.

1994–   London buses are now fully privatized, and
1996   Routemaster routes are retendered under individual contracts.

2000   Transport for London is created, bringing transport
       under the control of the elected Greater London
       Authority and the mayor, Ken Livingstone.
       Fifty additional Routemasters are bought and
       completely refurbished.
       Livingstone's bus supremo, Dave Wetzel, announces
       that discussions with manufacturers about a 'child of
       the Routemaster' have been initiated.

2003   Twenty routes with Routemasters remain. But on 29
       August Routemasters are removed from route 15, and
       from routes 11 and 23 in the following months.
       Sales of Routemasters resume.

2004   Transport for London announces its plans to make all
       of London's buses 'fully accessible' by the end of 2005.

2005   The last Routemaster makes its final journey on route
       159 from Marble Arch to Streatham. This last bus,
       RM2217, is driven by Winston Briscoe who came to
       Britain from Jamaica in 1962 and worked on the buses
       for 36 years. The last conductor is Lloyd Licorish who
       came to Britain from Barbados in 1965.

Appendix 2

ROOM FOR A LITTLE ONE INSIDE?:
THE JESTING CONDUCTOR

'Do you go near the Bank of England?'
'Only when I've got a great deal of money, sir.'

'Single to Paddington, please.'
'This bus doesn't go to Paddington, guv.'
'But it says "Paddington" on the front.'
'And it says India on the tyres, but we don't go there either.'

'Do you stop at the Ritz?'
'No lady, not on my wages.'

'What do I get for the Elephant?'
'Try buns.'

'Is this bus for the British Museum?'
'Not yet, guv.'

'Highbury Corner for Highbury tube, and all international destinations!'
'King's Cross for national rail and personal services!'

Appendix 3

THE ROUTEMASTERS' LAST JOURNEYS

159	Marble Arch – Streatham Station	9th December 2005
38	Victoria Station – Clapton Pond	28th October 2005
13	Golders Green Station – Aldwych	21st October 2005
14	Putney Heath – Tottenham Court Road Station	22nd July 2005
22	Putney Common – Piccadilly Circus	2nd July 2005
19	Finsbury Park Station – Battersea Bridge	1st April 2005
36	Queens Park Station – New Cross	28th January 2005
12	Notting Hill Gate – Dulwich Plough	5th November 2004
9	Hammersmith Bus Station – Aldwych	3rd September 2004
73	Victoria Station – Stoke Newington Common	3rd September 2004
390	Marble Arch – Archway	3rd September 2004
137	Streatham Hill – Oxford Circus	9th July 2004
7	Russell Square – East Acton Station	2nd July 2004
8	Bow Church to Victoria	4th June 2004
98	Willesden – Holborn Red Lion Square	26th March 2004
6	Aldwych – Kensal Rise	26th March 2004

94	Acton Green – Trafalgar Square	23rd January 2004
23	Liverpool St. Station – Westbourne Park	4th November 2003
11	Liverpool St. Station – Fulham Broadway	31st October 2003
15	Paddington Station – East Ham	29th August 2003

Heritage Routes

Since 15 November 2005 'Heritage Routemasters' have been running on these two routes 'between about 09:30 and 18:30':

15 Trafalgar Square – Tower Hill
9   Royal Albert Hall – Aldwych

ACKNOWLEDGEMENTS

My research has been drawn from various sources: interviews, stray conversations, periodicals, newspapers, pamphlets, reports, websites, films, newsreels and books. Much of the most interesting material (London Transport annual reports and press releases, journals, books, pictures, transcripts and ephemera) I discovered in the archives of London's Transport Museum in Covent Garden with the kindly assistance and knowledge of Helen Kent, Simon Murphy, Jonathan Riddell, David Bownes and Felicity Pemru.

Quotes in Chapter 9 from Reginald Rice and Charles Gomm are from transcripts of interviews conducted by Felicity Pemru on behalf of the Museum on 4 September 1991 and 22 July 1992. Permission is gratefully acknowledged.

I'd also like to salute the staff at the British Library in St Pancras and in Colindale, the London Library in St James and the Hulton Getty Archive, as well as the volunteers at the London Society.

I am immensely grateful to everyone at Granta. I am also grateful to all the bus people, conductors, drivers, engineers, enthusiasts, owners, Routemaster Association members and passengers who've spoken to me. Some of the names have, on request, been changed or omitted, but as I didn't find room to include all of the contributions I received, a quick thank you to those not already mentioned: Dennis Gimes of Holloway Garage, Bob at King's Cross, Ben Brook of the Save the Routemaster Campaign, Ernest Smith, Matthew Warmby, Theo Vereecken of the Dutch Routemaster Society and Philip Groves. On a more personal note, I couldn't have managed without the advice and support of Christine Kidney, Nick Rennison, Josh Lacey, Andy Miller, Chris Holifield, Nick Parker, Nicola Barr, Declan Clarke, Catherine Taylor, Kate Pemberton, Rachel Bailey, Paula Byerley Croxon, the folks and my partner, Lauren Wright, whose love sustained me throughout.

The inimitable Gail O'Hara produced some of the finest photographs in this book. View more of her work at *www.gailohara.com*.

I'd like to add a special thank you to Colin Curtis for his time, memories and hospitality, and to Andrew Braddock, an eloquent advocate for modern busing, who I hope will forgive me.

Travis Elborough
May 2005

ILLUSTRATION CREDITS

SOURCES

I would not have been able to write this book without numerous already existent accounts of the Routemaster and London's buses, transport and history. The bibliography below will point those who want to read more in the right directions.

Routemaster histories

Aldridge, J, Blacker, K, Booth, G et al. *The Birth of the Routemaster*. Harrow Weald: Capital Transport, 2004

Blacker, Ken. *Routemaster: Vol. 1, 1954–1969*. Harrow Weald: Capital Transport, 1991

Blacker, Ken. *Routemaster: Vol. 2, 1970–1989*. Harrow Weald: Capital Transport, 1992

Blake, J and Williamson, R J. *Routemaster Roundabout: A Silver Jubilee of Service 1956–1981*. London: Regent Transport Publishing, 1981

Brown, Stewart J. *Routemaster*. London: Ian Allan, 1984

Curtis, Colin. *The Routemaster Bus*. Tunbridge Wells: Midas, 1981

Curtis, Colin. *Forty Years with London Transport*. London: Transport Publishing, 1990

Morgan, Andrew. *Routemaster Handbook*. Harrow Weald: Capital Transport, 2001

Morgan, Andrew. *Working with Routemasters.* Harrow Weald: Capital Transport, 2004

Rixon, Geoff. *Routemaster.* London: DPR Marketing World of Transport, 1987

London transport and bus histories

Anon. *An Account of the Chiswick Works of the London General Omnibus Company.* London: London General Omnibus Company, 1922

Baker, Michael C. *London Transport 1933–1962.* Shepperton: Ian Allan, ·1996

Baker, Michael C. *London Transport Since 1963.* Shepperton: Ian Allan, 1997

Baker, Michael C. *London Transport in the 1950s.* Shepperton: Ian Allan, 2000

Barker, T C and Robbins, M. *A History of London Transport: Vol. 1, The Nineteenth Century.* London: Allen & Unwin, 1963

Barker, T C and Robbins, M. *A History of London Transport: Vol. 2, The Twentieth Century to 1970.* London: Allen & Unwin, 1974

Barker, T C. *Moving Millions: A Pictorial History of London Transport.* London: London Transport Museum, 1990

Blacker, Ken. *RT: The Story of a London Bus.* Harrow Weald: Capital Transport, 1980

Curtis, Colin and Townsend, Alan. *Chiswick Works: Building and Overhauling London Buses.* Harrow Weald: Capital Transport, 2000

Day, John R and Reed, John. *The Story of London's Underground.* Harrow Weald: Capital Transport, 2001

Glazier, Ken. *London Buses in the 1950s.* Harrow Weald: Capital Transport, 1989

Halliday, Stephen. *Underground to Everywhere: London's Underground Railway in the Life of the City.* Stroud: Sutton, 2001

Latchford, A H and Pollins, H. *London General: The Story of the London Bus 1856–1956*. London: London Transport, 1956

McCall, Albert William. *Greenline: The History of London's Country Bus Services*. London: New Cavendish Books, 1980

Moore, H C. *Omnibuses and Cabs: Their Origins and History*. London: Chapman and Hall, 1902

Murphy, C E. *London Buses: A Challenge from the Driver's Cab*. London: G T Foulis and Co, 1965

The Omnibus Society. *Vanguard: A Symposium: An Important Chapter in the Early History of the London Motor Bus*. London Historical Society, The Omnibus Society, 2001

Reed, John. *London Buses: A Brief History*. Harrow Weald: Capital Transport, 2000

Strong, L A G. *The Rolling Road: The Story of Travel on the Roads of Britain and the Development of Public Passenger Transport*. London: Hutchinson, 1956

Thomas, Alan. *AEC: Builders of London's Buses*. Hornchurch: I Henry, 1979

Wolmer, Christian. *The Subterranean Railway: How the London Underground Was Built and How It Changed the City Forever*. London: Atlantic, 2004

Design

Barman, Christian. *The Man Who Built London Transport: A Biography of Frank Pick*. Newton Abbott: David & Charles, 1979

Glancey, Jonathan. *Douglas Scott*. London: Design Council, 1988

Green, Oliver. *Underground Art: London Transport Posters 1908 to the Present Day*. London: Lawrence King, 2001

Green, Oliver and Rewse-Davies, Jeremy. *Designed For London: 150 Years of Transport Design*. London: Lawrence King, 1995

Loewy, Raymond. *Never Leave Well Enough Alone*. Revised edition. Baltimore: Johns Hopkins University Press, 2001

Documents

The Phelps Brown Report 1964, *Reshaping London's Buses 1966*

London Transport Annual Reports from 1947–1971, and press releases for the same period

Press notices issued by Transport for London since 2000

Customer Satisfaction with Articulated Buses, TfL Surface Transport Strategy and Business Development, June 2003

Magazines

Bus & Coach, November 1954

Buses, No. 564, March 2002

Buses Fayre, Vol. 6, No. 8, February 1984

Buses Illustrated, January/March 1955 and April/June 1956

Design, 418, October 1983

The Eagle, 22 June 1954

History Today, February 1998 (Doyle, Barry. 'Return of the Super Cinema')

London Transport Magazine, various issues from 1947 to 1971

Motor Transport, September–October 1954

Queen, 15 September 1959

Time, April 1966

Transit, May 2002

The Times, Illustrated London News, Daily Mail, Punch, Guardian, Metro and *Evening Standard* – various years

Albums

At the Drop of a Hat (Live), Flanders and Swann. Originally Parlophone, 1960. Reissued by EMI CDP7974652, 2003

Nancy in London, Nancy Sinatra. Originally Reprise, 1966. Reissued by Sundazed SC6054, 1995

Websites

Transport for London, London Buses Press Centre
www.tfl.gov.uk/buses/pn_home.shtml

Greater London Authority
www.london.gov.uk

The Routemaster Operators and Owners Association
www.routemaster.org.uk

Chiswick Park
www.enjoy-work.com/chiswick-park

London's Transport Museum
www.ltmuseum.co.uk

British Pathé news
www.britishpathe.com

Flanders and Swann Online
www.nyanko.pwp.blueyonder.co.uk/fas

Ensign Buses
www.ensignbus.com

Buses on Screen
www.busstation.net/screen/screen.htm

INDEX

Figures in *italics* indicate captions

CROSS RIVER TRAFFIC
A History of London's Bridges

Chris Roberts

Central London has seventeen points where the Thames can be strolled over, ranging from the fantastically fruity Tower Bridge to the grimly functional Wandsworth. *Cross River Traffic* covers a little history, facts and anecdotes of them all.

Vauxhall/London/Putney/Westminster/Blackfriars/Battersea/ Waterloo/Southwark/Hammersmith/Hungerford/Chelsea/ Lambeth/Albert/Wandsworth/ Tower/Millennium/

'Years of research and years of wearing out his shoes walking across the city's bridges has paid off . . . This book is packed full of great tales' *South London Press*

'Thousands of us cross London's bridges every day – on foot, by car, by train, or by cycle – yet who would ever look at them as objects of aesthetic value, let alone consider their history? Chris Roberts has done both in his fascinating new book' *What's on in London*

'An entertaining and well-illustrated book' *Canal Boat & Inland Waterways*

THE LIKES OF US
A Biography of the White Working Class
Michael Collins

The white working class are not seen as the loveable, apathetic Andy Capp characters they once were. They take to the streets when paedophiles and asylum seekers are in their midst; they expose their lives in TV documentaries; they love Gucci and hate the Euro. They are cast as racists by the liberal press, and the rightwing press mock their tastes and attitudes.

In *The Likes of Us* Michael Collins looks back at the intertwined history of his family and the working class area of Southwark where they have lived for generations to discover what remains of his class at a time of significant change.

'One of those rare books that make you swoon like the best pop singles used to' Julie Burchill, *Times* Books of the Year

'A fascinating blend of memoir and social history . . . a spiky defence of south London's white working class'
Blake Morrison, *Guardian*

'With *The Likes of Us*, Collins becomes an anatomist of England to dwarf almost all others . . . This is a passionate, humane, brave and beautifully controlled book, written in anger but not angrily written. Do what I did. Read it and weep'
Bryan Appleyard, *Sunday Times*

DOPE GIRLS
The Birth of the British Drug Underground
Marek Kohn

Dope Girls is about the transformation of drug use into a national menace. It revolves around the death in 1918 of Billie Carleton, a West End musical actress. Its cast of characters includes Brilliant Chang, a Chinese restaurant proprietor, and Edgar Manning, a jazz drummer from Jamaica. Around them in the streets off Shaftesbury Avenue and in Chinatown swirled a raffish group of seedy and rebellious hedonists. The drug problem was born, amid a gush of exotic tabloid detail.

'The best, most perceptive and most authoritative account of the British drug scene ever. This book is essential reading for doctors, legislators and law enforcers – indeed anyone who seeks to understand the impact that the illegal status of drugs has had on our society and culture' Will Self

'A rip-roaring read featuring flapper girls, Chinamen and "snow snifters", an eye-opening account of how fear about sex, race and class led to the criminalization of drugs' Amy Jenkins

'A fascinating look at cocaine and opium use in Britain after the first world war' Sarah Waters, *Sunday Times*

STET
An Editor's Life
Diana Athill

For nearly five decades Diana Athill helped shape some of the finest books in modern literature. She edited (and nursed and coerced and coaxed) some of the most celebrated writers in the English language, including V. S. Naipaul, Jean Rhys, Norman Mailer and Brian Moore. This candid and truthful memoir writes 'stet' against the pleasures, intrigues and complexities of her life spent among authors and manuscripts.

'A little gem . . . nostalgic, funny and valuable, written unashamedly for those who care about books' *Observer*

'This is a memoir of a life in publishing, and is written with a lovely and elegant lucidity' *Daily Telegraph*

'A narrative in which the passing literary stars take second place to an extraordinary guiding intelligence – sceptical, amused, humane' *New Statesman*

THE SILENT WOMAN
Sylvia Plath and Ted Hughes

Janet Malcolm

Is it ever possible to know 'the truth' about Sylvia Plath and her marriage to Ted Hughes, which ended with her suicide? In this brilliant, elegantly reasoned inquiry into the nature of biography, Janet Malcolm examines the various accounts of Plath's life, and the people who wrote them, to discover how Plath became an enigma in literary history, and why her legend continues to exert such a hold on our imaginations.

'Completely brilliant' David Hare

'Compulsively readable, the best thing Malcolm has ever done'
Elaine Showalter, *London Review of Books*

'Intellectually explosive, morally challenging and enormous fun'
Financial Times

WHEN I LIVED IN MODERN TIMES

Linda Grant

Winner of the Orange Prize for Fiction 2000.

It is April 1946. Evelyn Sert, twenty-years-old, a hairdresser from Soho, sails for Palestine, where Jewish refugees and idealists are gathering from across Europe to start a new life in a brand new country.

In the glittering, cosmopolitan, Bauhaus city of Tel Aviv, anything seems possible – the new self, new Jew, new woman are all feasible. Evelyn, adept at disguises, reinvents herself. Immersed in a world of passionate idealism, she falls in love, and with Johnny, her lover, finds herself at the heart of a very dangerous game.

'A novel that both stimulates the mind and satisfies the heart'
Scotland on Sunday

'Beautifully written, passionate . . . a deeply felt song of praise for Tel Aviv' *Sunday Times*

MY LIFE IN ORANGE
Tim Guest

'In 1980, at the age of six, Tim Guest was taken by his mother to spend his childhood in various communes of the Indian guru Bhagwan Rajneesh. This calm, meditative, and lyrical memoir is a testament to his recovery. Impressively, he is able to convey the spiritual longings and the political aspirations that impelled his mother and many other adults to risk so much in their quest for enlightenment and growth' Elaine Showalter, *Guardian*

'Tim Guest's extraordinary account of his childhood in the communes of Bhagwan, the notorious Indian guru, is a survivor's tale, poignant, funny and wise' Christopher Hart, *Sunday Times*

'This is the story of a very odd childhood. It is funny, gently ironic, closely observed, poignant and moving. Guest makes an astonishingly mature debut and has the rare ability to describe childhood as a small child lives it; accepting, helpless, curious. From his *Life in Orange* a very good writer has emerged. More will come, in whatever shade' Montagu Curzon, *Spectator*

RODINSKY'S ROOM

Rachel Lichtenstein with Iain Sinclair

David Rodinsky lived above the synagogue at 19 Princelet Street in the heart of the old Jewish East End of London. Sometime in the late sixties he disappeared. His room, a chaos of writings, annotated books and maps, gramophone records and clothes, was left undisturbed for twenty years. Rodinsky's abandoned room captured the imagination of a young artist, Rachel Lichtenstein, who became artist-in-residence there. Over a period of years she documented the bizarre collection of artefacts that she found there and became obsessed with this mysterious man. Lichtenstein and Iain Sinclair have written an extraordinary book that weaves together Lichtenstein's quest for Rodinsky – which took her to Poland, to Israel and around Jewish London – with Sinclair's meditations on her journey into her own past, and on the Whitechapel he has reinvented.

'Once you pick up this spell-binding book, you will have to read it straight through' *Sunday Times*

'A marvellous elegy for an East End rapidly being engulfed in scaffolding, concrete and cappucino bars' *Independent on Sunday*

THE SMOKING DIARIES
Simon Gray

When he turned sixty-five, the playwright Simon Gray began to keep a diary: not a careful honing of the day's events with a view to posterity but an account of his thoughts as he had them, honestly, turbulently, digressively expressed. *The Smoking Diaries* is the result.

'You should go out and buy *The Smoking Diaries* right now . . . you are unlikely to come across a funnier, cleverer, more painful book this year' Robert Hanks, *Daily Telegraph*

'Has a man ever written such sustained and hilarious diatribes against himself? His latest volume of diaries is a ramble – mad, maudlin, cross, nostalgic, despairing, and very, very funny' Craig Brown, *Mail on Sunday*

'Simon Gray's *The Smoking Diaries* is one of the funniest books I have ever read in my life' Philip Hensher, *Spectator*

'Simon Gray is our new favourite silver fox and the very definition of the word "louche"' *Guardian*

ALL THE DEVILS ARE HERE
David Seabrook

David Seabrook takes us on a deranged exploration of the depressing coastal towns of Thanet and the Medway covering Margate, Westgate, Rochester, Chatham, Broadstairs and Deal. He fuses his observation of these depression landscapes, city centres full of unemployed young men and asylum seekers and dodgy characters, with literary and historical associations that seem through his eyes more like bad dreams than heritage advertisements for the local tourist board. Written with high energy and seriousness, disturbingly personal and surprising, this is a unique book. There are devils here, and the reader will remember them.

'Narrative non-fiction is well served by David Seabrook's travels to the coastal dead zones of Thanet and Medway in north Kent, among the most shadowy and economically depressed areas in the whole of the British Isles, but which here provide a rich source of literary and art-historical reflection in the style of Iain Sinclair' *New Statesman*

'David Seabrook's debut work is a surreal exploration of the depressing reality of Kent's coastal towns. His observations are infused with a sense of the area's past literary incarnations that haunt the book and adds to the atmosphere of futility and fear' *The Times*

THE HARD SHOULDER
Chris Petit

'A former hard-man, O'Grady, returns after ten years in prison to the shabby part of North London where he used to live. Over the past decade, London has changed at a pace he finds difficult to cope with. The Irish community to which he once belonged has moved out of the area and many of the crooks and drinkers who were his friends have eased themselves into respectable middle age. As O'Grady comes to realize the extent of the gulf between himself and the world around him, he becomes more and more isolated . . . Chris Petit writes with confidence, inviting the reader to breathe the smoke and smell of stale beer in a marginal and hopeless world . . . he writes to great effect of the anger and loneliness of a man adrift in a world he does not recognize' *Times Literary Supplement*

'The prose has an understated, lilting beauty. *The Hard Shoulder* is a chill, crisp and eerie performance' *Scotland on Sunday*

'Petit has already established himself as an uncompromising observer of modern Britain; his iron-grey prose sets the mood of the times on those streets beautifully' *Big Issue*